History of the Eighty-sixth Regiment, Illinois Volunteer Infantry

History of the Eighty-sixth Regiment, Illinois Volunteer Infantry

and McCook's 36th Brigade
during the American Civil War

John R. Kinnear

LEONAUR

*History of the
Eighty-sixth Regiment,
Illinois Volunteer Infantry
and McCook's 36th Brigade
during the American Civil War*
by John R. Kinnear

First published under the title
*History of the
Eighty-sixth Regiment,
Illinois Volunteer Infantry*

Leonaur is an imprint
of Oakpast Ltd

ISBN: 978-0-85706-110-2 (hardcover)
ISBN: 978-0-85706-109-6 (softcover)

http://www.leonaur.com

Contents

To The
Commissioned Officers And Enlisted Men
Of The
Eighty-Sixth Regiment
Illinois Volunteer Infantry,
This volume is respectfully dedicated,
by The Author.

Preface

The history of the Eighty-sixth Illinois was written in part while the regiment was yet in the service, merely for the gratification of a personal desire; but since its muster out, the author has been frequently urged by many of his friends to have it published, that they might share what he alone enjoyed. He complied with an earnest request from Colonel Fahnestock to meet himself, General Magee, Major Thomas, Dr. Guth, Captain Zinser and others at Peoria, to have the manuscript examined before publication. It was met by their hearty approval, and an eager desire on their part to have it published; at the same time giving the assurance that they would lend their whole influence in getting it before the public. For these reasons the author has been induced to present this little volume to his comrades and friends, in the hope that it will receive their hearty welcome.

The history of the Eighty-sixth is also the history of the 85th, 125th and 110th Illinois, together with the 52nd Ohio and 22nd Indiana, all of the same brigade. Particular mention has been made of these regiments, for they were to the Eighty-sixth a band of faithful brothers.

The author acknowledges himself indebted to Colonel Fahnestock, Major Thomas, Captain Major, and Acting Adjutant Loveland, for the kind assistance and encouragement they have given him in preparing this history for publication, and to them he attributes the merit of this work, if it possesses merit.

The Author

CHAPTER 1

Organization, and March
to Nashville

The Eighty-sixth Regiment of Illinois Volunteer Infantry was organized at Peoria in the latter part of August, 1862. David D. Irons was made Colonel; David W. Magee, Lieutenant-Colonel; J. S. Bean, Major, and J. E. Prescott, Adjutant.

On the 26th of August the captains of the several companies drew lots for the letters of their companies, and on the next day the regiment was mustered into the United States service for the period of three years or during the war. On the 29th of the same month it received one month's pay, amounting to thirteen dollars. Nothing more of importance occurred until the 6th of September, when the regiment drew its guns and its first suit of army blue. While at Peoria the Eighty-sixth was rendezvoused at Camp Lyon, a name given it by Colonel Irons. Time passed slowly, for all were anxious to move to the seat of war, and were not at rest till they did. Finally, orders came, and on the 7th of September the regiment boarded the cars for Louisville.

Every member of the Eighty-sixth left Peoria with mingled feelings of pleasure and pain—pleasure, that they were about to participate in the great struggle for Union and Liberty—pain, that they were called upon to part with their nearest and dearest friends. It was on Sunday morning; beautiful and bright the sun shone upon its bristling armour as the regiment marched through the city with measured tread, bound for the "land of Dixie." The streets and balconies were filled with anxious friends, and fair hands waved us an affectionate *adieu*—hands which were not only true to us in our pride and strength, but also in the darkest hour of our trials and suffering. In long days after this,

11

when men turned copperheads by scores, these same *fair ones* proved true. "God bless the *fair!*" The regiment arrived in Jeffersonville, opposite Louisville, on the morning of the 9th, going into camp at Jo. Holt, on the Ohio river, across from the city of Louisville. At this camp the regiment first began to soldier, taking its first lessons in lying out in the open air. While at Jo. Holt it was drill, drill, almost constantly—the boys were not able to do enough drilling; but for all that, this camp became dear to us; especially in after times when water was scarce, memory would revert to the cool crystal waters of Jo. Holt.

After getting a partial outfit for campaigning, the regiment quit the Indiana side of the river, and crossed over to Louisville on the 14th. It again took up camp two miles south of the city in a very unpleasant situation, now remaining about Louisville until the 1st of October.

At one time, our brigade, which was formed on the 15th of September, and afterwards known as the 36th brigade of General Sheridan's division of Gilbert's corps, was marched through Louisville on grand review. This march was a severe one. The day was intensely hot and the roads dusty; then, the narrow streets made it doubly suffocating. Many fell powerless and died, and others received injuries for life. That day will long be remembered by those who were participators in its toils. The 85th and 125th Illinois, together with the 52nd Ohio regiment, were in the same brigade with the Eighty-sixth, and remained with it until all were discharged from the service at Washington City. The history of the Eighty-sixth Illinois is their history, and they were to each other as a band of brothers. Colonel Dan. McCook, of the 52nd Ohio, was placed in command of this newly formed brigade.

Soon after the formation of our brigade it made two other marches over the dusty roads in the direction of Bardstown, nearly as severe as the first one. They were doubtless unnecessary, and for that reason harder to perform, amounting to nothing, only out in the country ten or twelve miles and back again—training, no doubt. After these marches, the command was put in the rifle-pits that encircled the city of Louisville, for the Confederate army under General Bragg was near at hand menacing it. There was great excitement about this time, as we were unaccustomed to the work, and it went odd.

While remaining at Louisville, the Eighty-sixth went on picket for the first time. Its acts and thoughts on this occasion were certainly novel, and furnished a fund of great amusement in its after career. The regiment was just beginning to experience many of the roughs and cuffs incidental to the opening scenes of soldier life. Diarrhoea became a plague to many, and a change of diet a source of discomfort to others, which, upon the whole, caused us to lead a rather gloomy life at first; then we were ignorant of the many advantages an old soldier has acquired by long experience, which advantages greatly modify the hardships and discomforts of outdoor life.

While the regiment lay at Louisville, a large army was being brought together in order to oppose the encroachments of the enemy under Bragg, which had advanced as far as Bardstown. The forces on our part were commanded by Major General Buell, a man of questionable loyalty, as future events determined.

Finding that the enemy were not going to attack him, Gen. Buell issued orders for the advance of his whole command on the 1st day of October. Accordingly, the line of march was taken up at the time specified in the order, the 36th brigade being among the troops that went. As Buell's army advanced, the enemy retreated, taking with him large supplies from the country. Our forces followed rapidly for seven days, when Gen. McCook's command overtook a portion of Bragg's army at Chaplin Hills or Perryville. Here, on the next day, the 8th of October, was fought the desperate battle of Perryville.

The 36th brigade was on the left of the division and had moved forward early in the morning, accompanied by Barnett's 2nd Illinois battery, and occupied its position. The 85th Illinois, Colonel Moore, was deployed upon the right, and the 52nd Ohio on the left. The 125th Illinois, Colonel Harmon, was held as a reserve, and the 86th Illinois was on the picket line. At an early hour the rebel skirmishers opened a sharp fire on the 86th, and although this was the first fight in which, it was ever engaged, it advanced steadily upon them and drove them back in confusion with severe loss. Irritated at the loss of their position, the rebels massed upon the right and left, and commenced a furious fire from their batteries upon the brigade.

The firing continued for an hour, but the brigade resolutely held its ground. About this time Barnett's battery took position and silenced their guns. In the meantime, the 125th Illinois came to the support of the battery, and did its work splendidly, and the rebels retired, leaving the brigade in possession of the ground it had won.

A cavalry force now advanced in the direction the rebels were retreating, and were soon furiously attacked. The situation became critical. The cavalry was hard pressed, but with the assistance of the 2nd Missouri regiment, together with the 2nd Michigan and 15th Missouri, the enemy was completely routed at this point, making no other effort until 3 o'clock p.m., when General Bragg, in person, led his host against this position. After the most desperate fighting this last effort proved abortive.

From the commencement of this battle it grew fiercer and fiercer as the day advanced, and the sun of that day went down in blood. This was the first contest in which the 36th brigade was called upon to take a part, and though it was not as active as many others, it did promptly all that was required. Colonel McCook paid it high compliment for the soldierly manner in which it did its duty. The loss of the Eighty-sixth in this engagement was one killed and thirteen wounded. The battle of Perryville was evenly contested by the opposing forces, neither side having gained material advantage, though if there was a balance due either party, it was in favour of the Federals.

On the morning after the battle our brigade moved forward to the main portion of the battlefield, the enemy having retreated under cover of night, leaving his dead and wounded on the field. The brigade remained in its last position three days, when on the morning of the 12th the army took up the line of pursuit, passing through Danville and Lancaster, and arriving at Crab Orchard on the 16th. The pursuit was now no longer continued, the enemy being allowed to make good his escape with all his forage and plunder.

Nashville now became Gen. Bragg's objective point, making it a race to see which army could reach it first. Accordingly, on the 20th of October the line of march was taken up for Nashville, the 36th brigade passing back through Lancaster and Danville, thence following the main road leading to Bowling Green. It remained a few days near Mammoth Cave, in order to recruit its strength, being sorely fatigued. Many of the Eighty-sixth took this opportunity to see that great natural wonder. On the 31st of the month we arrived in Bowling Green, where the brigade remained a few days to recruit and draw clothing, preparatory to its further march. Leaving this place, it followed the main road to Nashville, where it arrived on the 7th of November.

The timely arrival of our army in Nashville relieved the anxious little garrison from further apprehensions of danger, and after so long a time the city was once more opened to communication. Here ended the arduous campaign against the forces of Gen. Bragg, the army being permitted to go into winter-quarters in and about Nashville.

The campaign just ended was one that tried the bone and muscle of the new levy of troops that had just entered the field. Water was very scarce, it being impossible to procure a sufficient quantity for our real good, and even that was of the most inferior kind; it was, in fact, unfit for a beast, and enough to sicken and kill a human. Our mode of cooking and eating then seems now to be ridiculous indeed; it was every man for himself, boiling his coffee in a pint tin and roasting his meat on a stick. Being barbarously ignorant of the profession of a soldier, we would carry unnecessary loads which we were afterwards taught to discard; and undergoing toilsome marches over a rough and desolate country, under the scorching rays of a Southern sun, with not enough water to wash down the dust we were compelled to breathe.

The men would readily push away the thick green scum from every stagnant pool and drink with a relish. Lazy swine were forced to leave their muddy beds to give place to the cup of the thirsty soldier. The Eighty-sixth Regiment in after times was wont to look back on this campaign—its first lesson in soldiering—with more commiseration and regret than any period of its subsequent career. It consumed thirty-eight days of the severest toils and privations, than which no other has surpassed, making a distance of over three hundred miles in pursuit of an exultant and defiant enemy.

The regiment now remained in Edgefield from the 7th of November until the 23rd, when it was marched to Mill Creek and took up encampment at a place known as Camp Sheridan. At this camp, on the 4th of December, at 12 o'clock m., the regiment having just returned from drill, was ordered to fall in and advance upon a force of the enemy's cavalry which was manoeuvring in the vicinity of the camp.

Company A and B were immediately thrown out as skirmishers; the remainder of the regiment kept back in reserve. The rebels were soon dispersed, and the regiment returned at night on the double-quick. On the 9th of December the command was marched to Nashville, taking up camp there, and put on duty about the city. About this time was led a sad and disagreeable life, even more so than at any other time. The boys were new in their profession and entirely ignorant as to what conveniences a soldier might have even under circumstances so trying, and in consequence, were compelled to render themselves most unhappy.

Some twenty odd men would live in the same tent, cook from a camp kettle swung in the middle of it, make their beds on the damp ground, frequently without even straw or boards under them. Snow fell, and the cold, keen winds of winter whistled without, while the poor soldiers lay cold and damp within.

Many were taken ill and died from this exposure; more died and were discharged during this winter than in all our previous and after term of service. The hospitals were yet without proper organization, the sick in them improperly cared for, for war was as yet a new thing, poorly understood and carried on. The Icelander, in his frigid and icy home of the far north, in his primeval ignorance, could not have lived in greater exposure than did the soldiers at this time.

The regiment was called upon to do a great deal of duty, such as picketing about the city—a business that is anything but pleasant where there are a number of generals and other fancy officers to be looked after. While on duty at this place the battles of Stone River were fought. There was an exciting time in Nashville during this eventful period; everything was hurry and bustle. The wounded and skulkers came back in great numbers, each bearing his own report.

During these battles the troops in and about the city had to be in line of battle at 3 o'clock in the morning; it mattered not what was the condition of the elements, it was all the same thing; and certainly, if anything would provoke a soldier to feelings of wrath, this kind of business would. The first one is to be heard from who ever got used to it.

On the 25th of March, 1863, the Eighty-sixth was marched to Brentwood, where only a few hours before the garrison there was surprised and captured. On the first alarm the regiment was sent to its assistance, but it reached the fatal spot too late, the rebels having succeeded in their enterprise and made good their escape. After this reconnoissance to Brentwood, the regiment returned to Nashville, settling down again to its old business of picketing and guarding. Nearly two weeks after this, on the 8th of April, the brigade was sent to Brentwood, in supporting distance of Franklin. Brentwood was a fine situation for a camp, and as spring was at hand it was rendered more pleasant still.

Comfortable quarters were readily made, and for the first time we began to live like men. It was here the boys began a happy reform in that respect; for instead of lying on the bare ground in the dirt and grass, they put up bunks, thus leading to their comfort. At this place the brigade built a fort called Fort Brentwood. It was triangular in form, having embrasures in the corners of the triangle for guns. Much time and labour was expended on this work, only to be completed that it might be demolished—a change in the situation of our army affairs compelling the evacuation of the fort. Details were made, and on the 3rd of June the work of demolition was consummated, and on the evening of the same day the brigade returned to Nashville.

The Eighty-sixth Regiment now remained in Nashville until the first of July, when it, with the rest of the brigade, was marched to Murfreesboro. At this encampment the command spent much time and labour on its camp grounds, but did not remain to reap the fruits thereof, for in a few days it returned to Nashville, where it remained until the 20th of August, 1863.

About this time occurred a sad epoch in the history of the Eighty-sixth Regiment—the death of Colonel Irons. After a severe illness he departed this life on the 11th day of August, leaving behind him a band of faithful friends to mourn his loss. Colonel Irons had the qualifications of a good man—a brave and faithful heart. On the day after his death the brigade escorted his last remains to the depot, where they were put on the cars and taken to Peoria for burial.

Soon after the death of Colonel Irons, Chaplain G. W. Brown offered his resignation, which was accepted on the 13th of October succeeding. Chaplain Brown gave his whole heart to the fulfilment of the duties incumbent on his office, by attending the sick and suffering of his regiment with a spirit and energy scarcely ever surpassed. He was indefatigable in his efforts to promote the happiness and welfare of his boys, and could always give inquiring friends from abroad the exact place and condition of the sick and suffering of the regiment.

CHAPTER 2

Battle of Chickamauga

On the 20th of August, 1863, Colonel Dan. McCook's brigade, belonging to Steedman's division of Granger's reserves, marched from Nashville in a southerly direction. The design of this move was to repair the Nashville and Decatur railroad. On its route the brigade stopped a short time at Brentwood, where it had been encamped some two months previous. Summer had made a vast change in this place. Fruits were ripe, and we partook freely, on the score of old acquaintance.

From Brentwood the brigade continued the march to Franklin, where it also remained a short time in order to complete the necessary arrangements to repair the railroad. Franklin is an old fashioned Southern town, and a place of much historic interest on account of the tragic scenes that have transpired there. Various battles have been fought there, and two notorious spies were hung. One regiment of the brigade was left at that place, and the rest strung along the road further down. The Eighty-sixth was stationed at West Harpeth, where it began getting out timber with which to repair a bridge.

Details were at work every day chopping and hewing, but it was not long till it received orders to discontinue the work and prepare for a march. West Harpeth is situated some eight miles south from Franklin in a fine portion of the country. The regiment was there in the fruit season of the year, enjoying soldier life in the first degree, for plenty sat smiling on every hand. And here it celebrated its first anniversary, Mr. Millsaps, who was afterwards its chaplain, delivering an address suitable to the occasion.

From West Harpeth the Eighty-sixth took up the line of march for Columbia. On its route it passed through Spring Hill, a very noted place. It was here that General Van Dorn, of the Confederate army, was shot for a gross insult extended to the wife of a prominent doctor.

On the evening of the 28th of August the regiment reached Columbia, Tenn., where it joined the brigade which had arrived there a short time previous, taking up quarters in the outskirts of the town until the 30th, when it was taken into it as a garrison. The remainder of the brigade continued the march in the direction of Huntsville, leaving the Eighty-sixth with orders to follow up as soon as relieved by a command of mounted infantry on its road from Kentucky. Columbia was a handsome place and of much interest. James K. Polk had lived there, and General Pillow's plantation was not far distant from it.

It had also several fine literary institutions, one of which continued in operation while the regiment was staying there. It was at Columbia Colonel Magee procured the famous whistle that ever afterwards remained with the regiment. By the mandates of this little instrument, in the hands of its successive commanders, the actions of the Eighty-sixth were controlled. It would advance, halt, retreat, lie down and get up, as designated by this tiny whistle. Other regiments have prided themselves in their eagles and pets, and the Eighty-sixth too, had long since concluded she "paid too dear for the whistle," not to cherish it in lasting remembrance. In years hence, when all things else will seem to have passed away, memory will not prove recreant to the faithful friend of all—the tiny whistle.

The regimental officers held an election here, and voted Captain A. L. Fahnestock Major of the regiment, though it was a long time after this before he was commissioned. The desired relief came on the 3rd of September, and the 86th took up the march on the 4th, following up the brigade, which by this time had reached Huntsville. The 28th Kentucky mounted infantry relieved us.

The weather was warm and the command marched slowly, feeling its way as it went. Colonel Magee did a good part by his men, always keeping their good and comfort in view; he would not compel them to overmarch themselves for personal gratification or that of his superiors, though always prompt in the execution of orders.

The regiment was now alone, surrounded by all manner of enemies. The brigade, on its passage down, was fired upon from houses in the little village of Lynnville, it now becoming a question whether a single regiment could make the passage at all. For the purpose of warding off all danger, the regiment observed the following order of march: One company two hundred yards in advance of the main column, and two companies in rear of the regimental train. It passed through Lynnville, the scene of former disturbances, without molestation, and camped near it.

Colonel McCook had issued an order to the citizens, declaring that for every life taken by concealed enemies he would retaliate on the country. This order had a good effect, for afterwards a citizen would not harbour a guerrilla or bushwhacker.

The members of the Eighty-sixth will not forget how they transcended the liberties of the colonel, while camped at Lynnville, by killing hogs in camp, and raising "Ned" generally—the lecture they received in consequence will not be forgotten. He admonished them never to permit a rebel hog to be too insinuating without the proper chastisement, and at the same time not to be too noisy and reckless, thus exposing him to the reprimand of his superiors.

The next place of encampment was at Pulaski, a small town that lay almost in ruins from some cause or other. A novel incident occurred here respecting a couple of doctors. The first one tried to elude the advance guard by riding off in break-neck style, but he was apprehended, brought before Colonel Magee, and examined. He declared his object to be to save his favourite pony and nothing more; he was of course released, but on further suspicion of being a spy, was searched for, but could not be found.

The other doctor came into camp of his own accord, and going to the surgeon's tent, asked for a dose of morphine; whereupon, seeing a good opportunity, he stole the whole bottle, and putting it in his hat walked off. He was detected, arrested, and taken before the Colonel. He plead insanity and such like things to no purpose, but was tied up to a tree and made to suffer punishment. No one can rightly determine the object of these two men; they were doubtless enlisted sons of the Southern chivalry intent upon mischief.

The march was continued the next day from Pulaski, crossing Elk river at a place known as Elktown, the boys dismantling themselves and wading, as the bridge had been destroyed. Four miles beyond this stream is the State line, the regiment marching there and camping for the night near a beautiful brook of water.

On the 7th of September, it crossed the line and camped twelve miles south of it. The next day it reached Huntsville, and passing through, took up quarters in the outskirts. The Eighty-sixth was the only Union troops in the vicinity, the brigade having passed on, leaving orders for it to follow immediately. When night came on, the colonel became uneasy, for citizens reported a force of the enemy near at hand. Upon this intelligence he moved his command into town, and took up position on the square. Companies were stationed in the different streets leading to it, in anticipation of a surprise. The night passed in suspense, but no enemy appeared.

Huntsville was a beautiful town with a fine location. It was, before the war, the mart of Northern Alabama. There is a large and handsome spring there, well worth the visit of the tourist and passer-by. By its own force it runs machinery which pumps water for the whole town in sufficient quantity.

The regiment greatly disliked to leave this place, and, in after times, when it was wont to wish itself in some pleasant abode, it would fondly revert to Huntsville. But, early on the morning of the 10th, it took up the line of march for Stevenson, Alabama, where it expected it would certainly join the brigade. It had not marched from Huntsville more than three miles when a soldier from Company H, Mr. Church by name, while walking in the woods near the road, espied a squad of concealed bushwhackers, whereupon he fired at them, and killed one. The dead body was brought to the road and left in plain view, being labelled with these words: "A bushwhacker." A great number of negroes—men, women and children, of every age and size, of every hue of the skin from yellow to concentrated blackness, followed out from Huntsville, presenting a jolly scene.

The march to Bridgeport attaches nothing of much importance to it, only the usual occurring incidents. The sick and barefooted were left at Brownville, to be transported from thence to Stevenson on the cars, where they joined the command. The regiment reached Bridgeport on the 14th, where it received a mail—he first since Columbia. The brigade had gone on from this place to Chattanooga, to join General Rosecrans' army, which was on the eve of battle with Bragg.

On the morning of the 15th, the regiment left Bridgeport, and on the evening of the 16th, tired and worn out, it crossed Lookout mountain, and joined the brigade at Rossville, six miles south from Chattanooga. In this vicinity was collected a large army, and the great battles that succeeded were imminent. Here ended these hard marches after so long a time. The Eighty-sixth had been in the campaign nearly twenty-seven days, seventeen of which it formed its own company, having passed over the hostile country lying between Columbia and Chattanooga, which was infested with strong bands of guerrillas of the most desperate kind, without the loss of a man. It was now much fatigued and hoped to have a short respite from its labours—but not so, something of a more terrible nature was forthcoming—the bloody battle of Chickamauga.

General Bragg turned on our forces under Rosecrans, on the 16th of September, on the 17th, skirmishing began, and on the 18th, very hard skirmishing and some fighting came off. It was on the 18th that the brigade, under command of Colonel Dan. McCook, was sent out to the Chickamauga Creek to burn a bridge, which it successfully accomplished. A force of the enemy came near capturing it, having nearly surrounded it. During the fight that ensued, it lost a good many men. On the evening of the 19th, the brigade returned to Rossville, afterwards moving out on the road leading to McAfee Church, and took up position just inside the Rossville Gap. Here it remained in readiness for any emergency, all the night of the 19th.

Our corps, commanded by General Gordon Granger, was held in reserve at this battle, and was not generally engaged on the 19th. The battle of the 19th was a hard contested one, and, when night came, the advantages were about equal. The enemy were vastly superior in numbers, in about the ratio of five to three, making him buoyant and desperate on this day and the next. On the next day, the 20th of September, the fate of Chickamauga was to be decided.

The battle commenced at half-past eight a.m., the effort of the enemy being, as on the previous day, to turn the left flank of our army, and then gain access to the Lafayette and Chattanooga road. Thomas, who was in command at the left, was hard pressed from the start, and General Rosecrans directed him to hold on, assuring him that he should be reinforced if necessary, by the entire army. Our brigade was moved, early on the morning of the 20th, from its position of the night previous, and marched out on the left wing of the army to an old church, known as the McAfee Church.

Here it manoeuvred about on the left flank of the army, taking different positions, in readiness for the expected advance of the enemy in that quarter. The battle continued to rage furiously on our right. From some misunderstanding, there was a gap left in the line of battle on the right centre of the army. The rebels instantly worked into this breach, striking our troops in flank and rear, throwing them into complete confusion, from which they never recovered till they reached Rossville. Seven brigades, or about one-fourth of our entire force, were thus swept away by this misfortune, and though the loss in killed and wounded was not very heavy, and that in prisoners less than would have been expected, they were effectually cut off from rendering further aid to the rest of the army during that day.

Among those in this rout, were, without fault of their own, Major-Generals Rosecrans, McCook, and Crittenden. Each made repeated efforts to join the main body, but in vain, and finally fell back to Rossville, whence General Rosecrans sent his chief of staff, General Garfield, to ascertain how Thomas was succeeding in holding the rebels at bay, and himself, with Generals McCook and Crittenden, went on to Chattanooga, to secure the trains and put the city in a state of defence, if, as he feared, the army should be driven to retreat thither. The rout on the right wing took place about one o'clock p.m.

Notwithstanding the break on the right, General Thomas, though opposed by a force at least five to two, stood grim and defiant, resisting the repeated assaults upon his lines with a persistency never surpassed. From two o'clock till sunset, a terrible battle raged along Thomas' line. About two in the afternoon, our brigade was ordered to the assistance of Thomas, it then being some three miles to his left, and going this distance on the double-quick. The General saw a cloud of dust in the direction we were coming, and, it is said, he was uneasy at first, not knowing whose forces they were, Confederate or Union. A messenger was sent to ascertain who they were and whence they came.

When the brigade arrived and was taking up position, the enemy opened a furious fire upon it, and had it advanced a short distance further, would certainly have been captured. When the brigade got into position, Battery I, replied with spirit to the fire of the enemy, which, by this time, had got the right range on us. Our position now became fairly hideous; the woods roared and the very heavens quaked, while shot and shell filled the air with frightful sounds. The grass and woods between our brigade and the enemy had caught fire, which conspired to make our position more disagreeable than ever, though it doubtless saved us a hard fight, for the rebels would not advance through it.

The other two brigades of our division, still on our right, led by General Steedman in person, rushed upon the enemy in a furious charge, which was passing through a low gap to the rear and flank of Brannan's position. The shock was terrible; and for a time, as the opposing forces met in a hand-to-hand fight, success swayed from side to side; in a few minutes more the enemy was repulsed, and dared not make the attempt again. A thousand of these brave men fell, killed or wounded, in that brief half hour's struggle; but they held the gap.

When night came, the battle ceased, everything becoming still and

23

hushed. The enemy now fell back, leaving the field of battle in possession of General Thomas; but finding the ammunition, food and water necessary for his men were exhausted, the General withdrew with his troops about midnight to Rossville, where they arrived in good order.

McCook's brigade was the last that left the field, and the Eighty-sixth, the last regiment. It was after one o'clock at night when it passed the Rossville Gap and went into camp. There laid down to sleep that night a tired set of men, the fatigues of the day having almost overcome them. Many a brave comrade fell on the bloody field of Chickamauga; and another such would have ruined our army.

On the next day, the 31st, our brigade took a position on the right of Rossville Gap. A strong force was left here to keep back the enemy till the army could fall back on Chattanooga. The rebels pushed buoyantly forward and opened on us a heavy cannonade. Our forces held the gap until night, when they abandoned it, and retreated on Chattanooga. Our brigade arrived in Chattanooga very late at night, and after much changing about, took up position and laid down to rest.

Here ends the battle and the retreat, a stirring epoch in our history. During this battle, the regiment had the honour of conducting itself in a praiseworthy manner. There is but one exception, and that is personal. It was the case of Major O. Fountain, who conducted himself in a disrespectful manner by becoming intoxicated. On this account he was soon afterwards recommended for a discharge, which was duly furnished him. Major Fountain had many qualifications of a good soldier, and previous to this, had conducted himself in a proper manner.

After the battle, our brigade remained in Chattanooga three days, during which time it was formed in line and held as a reserve. The enemy was hourly expected to pounce upon our forces and attempt to regain the place, for unless they did, no real advantages were gained by their successes at Chickamauga. Our troops were not disheartened or hopeless, but eager and determined to conquer in a second engagement. The enemy, however, was severely punished, otherwise he would have followed up his successes.

CHAPTER 3

Mission Ridge and Knoxville

On the 24th of September, four days after the battle of Chickamauga, our regiment and brigade was ordered to the north side of the Tennessee river, to guard a ford near the mouth of North Chickamauga Creek, some eight miles up the river from Chattanooga.

On its way to this ford, the brigade remained a few days near another ford about equidistant from the upper one and Chattanooga, where it threw up works, and leaving the One Hundred and Twenty-fifth Illinois to guard them, went on to the upper ford, arriving there on the 27th, and taking up permanent quarters. This place was considered a prominent one in a military view, and was accordingly strongly protected.

The boys now set to work building shanties for their comfort, as it was probable the command would make its winter-quarters there. They would fell trees, chop off large cuts and split them into slabs. Out of these rough slabs snug shanties were made, and to put on the finishing touch, fire-places were built in them. When cold, keen winds blew fierce without, the soldier sat comfortable within, and soon our North Chickamauga camp became a semi-paradise—a home in the woods. It was here the brigade suffered so much from hunger; famine was our ghost, it haunted us by day and by night.

The troops were not supplied with half rations, for the transportation of the army was insufficient. It was impossible to procure adequate supplies for a large army by hauling them sixty miles over the horrible roads across the Cumberland and Walden ridges—roads in which six miles a day was all the distance a six-mule team could accomplish. This state of affairs could not last long.

The Tennessee River is very crooked. Below Chattanooga it makes two bends; the first, eight miles in circuit, and only one and a half across; the other, thirty miles in circuit, and four miles across. If these two peninsulas could be gained, wagon transportation would be reduced to ten miles. To accomplish this, Hooker's command was ordered from Bridgeport through Shellmount to the Lookout Valley, thence to Brown's Ferry. While Hooker was doing this, a detail from Chattanooga, under command of General Hazen, proceeded down the river in pontoon boats to Brown's Ferry, and succeeded in laying a pontoon bridge.

From here there was a good road to Kelly's Ferry, and loaded wagons could go from that point to Chattanooga in half a day.

On the night of the 27th, General Geary's division of Hooker's command, pitched its camp in advance of the main force, near Wauhatchie in the Lookout Valley, and was attacked at two o'clock on the morning of the 28th.

Geary held his ground, and Longstreet was defeated with severe loss. The night of this battle was clear, and the moon shone bright. The roar of artillery and rattle of musketry could be distinctly heard from our camp on the Chickamauga. Such an affair at the dead of night, when all else is calm and hushed, presents a thrill of emotions that can be experienced under no other circumstances.

On the 29th of October, Colonel Dan. McCook received orders to despatch two of his regiments to the assistance of General Hooker, who was now in the Lookout Valley. The Eighty-sixth Illinois and Fifty-second Ohio, were accordingly ordered to report to him. They crossed to the south side of the Tennessee on the pontoon bridge at Kelly's ferry, below Chattanooga. After crossing the river, the Eighty-sixth was sent to guard a pass in the Raccoon ridge, and passed there a most miserable night. It was perched on a hill-side, the rain falling in torrents, and every man being obliged to hold to a sapling to keep from going down.

From this pass, the next day, the regiment went down the ridge to a position opposite Lookout Mountain, where it relieved a brigade of Hooker's men. The enemy had a battery planted on the Lookout, at the Point of Rocks, whence he shelled us continually. The boys could tell when this battery would shoot, and dodge accordingly. It was here we had our first intercourse with Eastern troops. They had odd ways, peculiar to themselves, which the Western boys were unused to, and in consequence, many taunting words were passed, for either party was loath to take the jaw of the other.

The Eighty-sixth and Fifty-second, remained in front of Lookout

Mountain five days, when they were relieved and sent back to North Chickamauga, arriving there on the evening of the 5th of November, after an absence of seven days.

Again the boys set themselves to refitting their shanties, for it now seemed probable there would be no more moving for a long time. The weather was then disagreeably cold, and they must work or freeze-they worked.

Most every mess soon had comfortable habitations, and some of them very neat ones indeed. But after all their pains, it became evident they would not remain long at this camp. Our army was beginning to strengthen, and everything indicated a move.

About the 20th of November, pontoons were placed in the mouth of the North Chickamauga for some purpose, then unknown, but afterwards revealed. There were one hundred and sixteen pontoon boats in number, in which Giles A. Smith's brigade of the Fifteenth Corps embarked on the night of the 23rd, and entering the Tennessee, moved swiftly down three miles, closely hugging the right bank; then crossed, and landed a small force above the West Chickamauga, and the remainder just below it. Landing this force, the boats were dispatched to the opposite side for reinforcements. Two divisions were ferried over, and by noon, a pontoon bridge across the Tennessee, fourteen hundred feet long, and another across the West Chickamauga, two hundred feet long, were completed.

Long before daylight on the morning of the 24th, our division under command of Jefferson C. Davis, was marched down the right bank of the Tennessee to a point opposite the mouth of the West Chickamauga, where the pontoon bridge was being constructed. At one p.m., the Fifteenth Corps, on the left bank of the river, advanced in three columns, and at half-past three were in possession of the Missionary Hills without loss. Our division crossed the pontoons late in the afternoon of the 24th, in a drizzling rain, and after much manoeuvring took up a position in a thick and swampy woods.

The night of the 24th passed off with some fighting, as the enemy made an effort to regain his lost ground, but his effort proved abortive. During the battle of the 25th, our division was held as support to General Sherman, who was ordered to make a demonstration on Fort Buckner, on Tunnel Hill. When Sherman's persistence had drawn nearly one-half the force from Fort Bragg to Fort Buckner, six signal guns, fired at intervals of two seconds, told the advance of the Fourth Corps to the assault on Fort Bragg.

27

This assault proved a complete success. The rebel works were captured, and with Hooker on their left flank and rear, and their centre broken, they were in a complete rout. Here ended the day, and under cover of night Bragg's army beat a hasty and disorderly retreat.

During this battle our brigade was not engaged, but being held in close reserve, it could see things well done. The next thing on the programme was the pursuit. Our division was ordered to march at one o'clock a.m., on the 26th, and crossing the Chickamauga by the pontoon at its mouth, pushed forward for the enemy's depot, and by eleven a.m. it appeared at the depot, just in time to see it in flames. Entering with one brigade, General Davis found the enemy occupying two hills partially entrenched, just beyond the depot. They were soon driven away. At this place was to be found all manner of things, burning and broken. Corn and corn-meal, wagons, caissons, guns, pontoons, balks, chesses, and the like, were lying around promiscuously.

As the command advanced, every kind of plunder lined the road, the private soldier having even thrown away his provisions and clothing, being in the utmost confusion and excitement. When the division reached Shepherd's run, some two miles north of Grayville, it found the enemy's rear guard intending to camp, and showing a disposition for fight. Accordingly, General Davis ordered it into line and to charge the rebels away. It was not long in executing orders. After running a long distance, jumping fences, creeks and other obstacles, it found the enemy in strong skirmish force, which was made to give ground, but night drawing near, no decisive advantage was gained.

Our division held its position until morning, when it was again set off on the pursuit, marching in supporting distance of General Hooker who was engaging the enemy at the Ringgold pass. After several charges, Hooker finally succeeded in dislodging the rebel force, and took possession, capturing three hundred prisoners. The loss of Hooker's command here was heavier than in the capture of Lookout mountain.

The junction of Bragg and Longstreet was now no longer a possibility. In the meantime, the siege of Knoxville was pressed with ardour by the forces under Longstreet, and Burnside found himself in close quarters. Having disposed of Bragg, General Grant determined to send a force, under Sherman, to the relief of Knoxville. Our division formed a part of this force.

Early on the 28th of November, bleak and cold, Sherman began his northern march through East Tennessee, to the assistance of the beleaguered city. On its route to Knoxville, our division passed near Cleveland on the 29th, and on December 1st, crossed the Hiawassee river. Marching on, it arrived at a point on the Little Tennessee opposite Morgantown, on the 4th, and crossing, marched up the river four miles when orders were countermanded; then, countermarching, recrossed the river at Morgantown—Longstreet having abandoned the siege, and hastily retreating towards Virginia.

The object of the expedition now being accomplished, the army began its return march on the 7th of December. General Jeff. C. Davis had orders to march to Columbus by way of Madisonville. On its return, the division passed through Madisonville, on the first day's march, leaving the Eighty-sixth Illinois to garrison it during the night. The regiment lived well while here, nearly every family being set to work baking corn-bread, cakes, and such. It passed a pleasant night with the good folks of this inland village, only regretting that it could not remain longer and enjoy more of their forced hospitality.

Leaving Madisonville, the regiment plod on after the division, marching the distance of twenty-five miles, through mud and rain, reaching the Conasauga Mills about ten o'clock on the night of the 8th, when the division was encamped. No Eighty-sixth man will be so recreant to the memories of the past as to forget this day's march. And no one will forget the manly action of our colonel on this occasion, who, to encourage his men, trudged along through mud and rain, allowing his wearied boys to ride his horse by turns. The division remained encamped near these mills one week, living fat on corn-meal, molasses and pork.

On the 15th, it again took up the march, bound for Chattanooga, and arrived there in the afternoon of the 18th, after a toilsome march. Our brigade was detained several hours, waiting to be ferried over the Tennessee. It was very late at night when the Eighty-sixth effected a crossing, and when once over, it camped for the remainder of the night, marching up to its old camping ground, on the morning of the 19th.

Here ends the Knoxville campaign, and the Eighty-sixth back in its old camp on the North Chickamauga. This campaign consumed twenty-five days of the severest marching and suffering that ever soldiers experienced. Many returned barefooted and threadbare, in the chill month of December, leaving bloody tracks on the frozen ground. This march may be fairly numbered among the hardest of our hardships. No men ever bore up under so many ills with more fortitude than did the men in this arduous and difficult campaign to the relief of the besieged and almost subjugated Knoxville. On this trip we saw more loyal people than in all our previous service.

Long live the good people of East Tennessee; may they live in peace and die in plenty!

On this march Company G, of the Eighty-sixth, met with a sad misfortune near Louden; it was the accidental death of Sergeant Haynes. The column had just halted when one of his company carelessly threw down his gun, which going off, shot the sergeant in the head, killing him instantly.

The boys now made free to stick close to their shanties and fire-places, for their clothing was scant and the weather extremely cold. The division did not remain at North Chickamauga long, for, on the 26th of December, it crossed the Tennessee, taking up camp at McAfee's church, on the left of the Chickamauga battlefield and six miles from Chattanooga.

CHAPTER 4

About Chattanooga

The beginning of the year 1864 found the Eighty-sixth regiment in camp at McAfee's church, busily engaged in building shanties and preparing for the winter, which was extremely cold and disagreeable. These rude habitations were soon made comfortable, and had we been well provided with provisions and clothing, everything would have passed off gay and lively. Eighteen hundred and sixty-three passed away, taking with it many fond recollections, and many, too, that were not pleasant. The hardships and privations we were called upon to endure, together with our successes and pleasures, seemed now to be nothing more than an apologue of which the moral is the only reliable feature. There was good cause for rejoicing, for success had attended our arms on land and sea. The Mississippi had been opened, and the enemy amazingly defeated at every point in the South-west.

Our encampment on the Chickamauga battle-ground had a fine location, and possessed many advantages in wood and water. A deal of pains and labour was taken to make this camp comfortable and healthy. Green trees were set out in front of the company grounds, which beautified and made them enchanting.

This vicinity of the South is noted for its grand natural scenery, nowhere to be surpassed. We read of the romantic scenery of the Oriental world—of the versatility of Italia's summer winds—of the magic charms of her hills, her rills, and dales; but the realities here presented are more enchanting than the probabilities of a might be in other parts of the world. From the heights of Lookout Mountain the country around has the appearance of one vast field of ridges, tending in their direction from north to south. This mountain is 2,500 feet above the level of the Tennessee, and from the Point of Rocks, a man in the valley below appears to be no larger than one's thumb, and a train of cars gliding along at its base has the appearance of tiny toys. Chattanooga, a distance of more than five miles, seems to lie directly at its base. The first range of ridges to the eastward of Lookout range is known as Missionary Ridge. The next in succession are the Pea Vine, Pigeon, Taylor's, and Rocky Face.

Missionary Ridge, the scene of Bragg's disaster, breaks off from its regular course at Rossville, in a curve to the eastward, striking the river some five miles above Chattanooga, thus forming on the south and south-east a perfect wall of natural defenses, upon which, for two months, lay the besieging forces of the Confederate army. To complete the semicircle of walls around Chattanooga on the south side of the river, Lookout mountain stands in its huge dimensions, a key to the South-west.

In the Chickamauga valley, on the south-east side of Missionary Ridge, from McAfee's church to Lee and Gordon's Mills, is the site of the Chickamauga battlefield.

That place, even when we went there to camp, more than three months after the battle, presented a repulsive sight. The enactment of that terrible conflict, when leaden rain fell thick and fast around us, when the dying were gasping in the last agonies of death, when wounded and dead men covered the gory field, and the terrible thought of immediate danger crowded our minds,—produced not half the emotions of human misery that were experienced nearly four months afterwards when we viewed the same field. Here and there could be seen the putrefied form of a human creature in Union garb. Sometimes the skull and other members of the body were seen detached along the roadside or on a stump, having been taken from their peaceful repose by ruthful hands or hungry dogs.

The entire field was yet cumbered with great numbers of our dead, and, in most cases, the flesh had fallen from the bones, leaving nothing but the mere skeleton. Years hence, children yet unborn will find, in their sports upon this field, a skull or a bone of these poor victims, and wonder and ask what it is; then, some grandfather will tell them of the great battle of Chickamauga.

But to return to Camp McAfee. For awhile at first, the boys were obliged, in a measure, to furnish their own supplies. Every day, some one of each mess had to go six miles to mill and try his hand for flour, sometimes being extremely lucky, but more frequently, to return without a mite. These were, with propriety, called our "milling days." Thus our time dragged heavily on.

On the evening of the 27th of January, our division received orders to march the next morning at daylight, with three days rations in their haversacks. Accordingly, on the morning of the 28th, it led out in the direction of Ringgold, still under the command of General Jeff. C. Davis. General Batie's brigade followed Morgan's, and Colonel McCook's brought up the rear. The evening of the same day the command camped at Ringgold, a distance of twelve miles.

Here it remained until ten a.m. the next day, waiting the result of a reconnoissance which was being made in the direction of Tunnel Hill, when it returned to McAfee. The enemy was found in force at that place, and his strength tolerably well ascertained, which was the real object of the expedition. This reconnoissance resulted in the capture of forty prisoners, besides five killed and seventeen wounded.

Again, on the 14th of February our brigade marched to Chickamauga Station to relieve the 1st brigade which was there on outpost duty. The weather was now cold and wet, and we were without shanties, but the boys, with their usual energy, set to work and soon constructed comfortable quarters. The houses in the vicinity of the camp were made to suffer badly; in many instances not even a nail was left to mark the spot where once stood a neat frame building. Colonel Magee returned to his regiment while it was here, having been home on furlough, every one being glad to see his familiar face. About the time we began to realize the benefit of our labours at this place, the brigade was ordered to march, having been there eight days. On Tuesday morning, the 23rd, the brigade received orders to march in one hour's time, it being reported that the lines would not advance further than Grayville, and there go into camp.

In consequence of this understanding, almost every soldier carried a huge load of camp plunder; but they were sadly mistaken, since the column marched rapidly on Ringgold, a distance of sixteen miles, where the other two brigades of the division had previously arrived. Most of the command became so much fatigued under their burden that they were obliged to fall out and come up at their leisure.

On the next day the division continued the march from Ringgold through Tunnel Hill on to Buzzard's Roost, a narrow defile in the Rocky Face Ridge, where it found the enemy in force and very defiant. On reaching the position of the enemy at this place, our brigade was drawn up in line of battle, advancing into position so as to cover the pass, during which time a heavy cannonade was opened on our lines, and continued until dark. General Morgan's brigade having taken up position on our left, pickets were now sent out, and comparative silence prevailed during the night.

Companies E and H were detailed from the Eighty-sixth for picket duty on this occasion, company A being sent on the skirmish line the next day at 12 m.

On the morning of the 25th the pass was enveloped in a dense fog, so much so that objects could not be distinguished at any great distance, it being impossible to discover a vestige of the enemy's lines until about ten a.m., when the fog had partially disappeared. About this time, however, skirmishing began along the line, resulting in a few serious casualties on our part.

The main reason for delaying operations so long was in not knowing the exact situation of General Cruft, who had been sent round the left of Rocky Face Ridge in order to flank the enemy's position at Buzzard's Roost Gap. Cannon could be heard in that direction booming furiously, but nothing definite could be determined by that.

It soon became evident, however, that he was advancing rapidly on their flank and rear, since the roar of the cannon and rattle of musketry became more and more distinct; but no news came respecting his progress until about ten a.m., when an orderly arrived with the desired information. Towards noon the fog disappeared, and the sun having risen high, made it more favourable for operations, since in the morning it shone in our eyes and blinded us.

About one o'clock, Hotchkiss' 2nd Minnesota and Warren's 19th Indiana batteries moved into position in front of our brigade on a high eminence, from whence they began to feel for the position of the enemy, which was soon discovered strongly fortified on the adjacent hills. Soon after this the Eighty-sixth was ordered to advance over the hill on which these batteries were stationed, and attack the enemy's position.

When it reached the crest of the hill, the rebels opened a furious fire upon it, but this did not derange the line one particle, it marching on with as much good order as if on battalion drill. The regiment advanced to the foot of a hill or ridge only a few hundred yards from the enemy's line of works, where it halted and lay down. Colonel McCook urged Magee to charge the works, but he would not until he got support on his right, as it was unprotected, and would have resulted in the utter ruin of the regiment.

The 85th, it is true, was on the right of the Eighty-sixth, but not in supporting distance, having partially changed its direction and ascended the acclivity on the right too high. At the same time our brigade advanced on the right, General Morgan advanced on the left and made a desperate charge on the enemy's position; but he was repulsed in great disorder, the steep and rugged rocks affording a natural barrier against his assaulting force. The charge on the left having failed of success, the right was ordered to maintain its own, it being the design, however, to push forward the right had Morgan succeeded in his enterprise.

The Eighty-sixth remained in its position until night, when it was relieved by other troops, and falling back to the rear, remained in comparative quiet during the night.

On the morning of the 26th the Eighty-sixth was marched to a position covering the right flank of our forces in the gap. It was anticipated that a force of the enemy's cavalry would make a demonstration in that direction. Here the regiment built good breastworks in readiness for the expected attack; but no enemy came, though it remained until night, when it was withdrawn, taking up the line of march for Ringgold. Soon after this the whole force was put on the retreat, arriving in Ringgold late at night.

Every Eighty-sixth man will remember the odd sight that occurred on this retreat as it entered Tunnel Hill. A large frame building had caught on fire and was in full blaze when we entered town. While descending a ridge in closed ranks, the light from the burning building was reflected from every face, presenting a multitude of bright, pleasing countenances, and as all else was dark, nothing could be seen but a moving field of shining faces.

Our brigade was not generally engaged in the battle just recited, the Eighty-sixth and the 85th Illinois being the only regiments brought into action, though the rest were in close reserve. The Eighty-sixth loss was one killed and seven wounded, the company loss being as follows: Co. H, three; Co. G, one; Co. K, four. The reconnoissance was now ended, and its objects accomplished.

The rebels had been sending troops to Mobile, but the movements of this expedition compelled them to bring them back. On the next day, the 27th, the division was put on the march for Camp McAfee, where it arrived at dusk of the same day, having been absent thirteen days. But after all, we were destined to remain here only a short time. Just one week after the reconnoissance to Buzzard's Roost we were again put on the move.

Our brigade received orders to march on Sunday, the 6th day of

March, to Lee and Gordon's Mills, situated on the right of the Chickamauga battle-ground, about eight miles distant from the camps at McAfee. The command was sent here on account of this being a strategic point, and soon began to lay off a camp, which day by day it adorned and beautified until it became an enchanting place, the very prototype of the grand and beautiful, being situated on the banks of the South Chickamauga, a handsome stream of water.

When good comfortable shanties had been erected, the boys began to ornament their grounds after the first order of things, for neither time nor labour was spared in this work, each soldier taking a pride in doing his part. All the companies of each regiment fabricated ornaments of every conceivable workmanship, differing one from another, and on the whole really handsome. These ornaments were made of pine and cedar boughs by the more dextrous and artistical of our comrades. You might see well-fashioned eagles, letters, figures and animals hung up in conspicuous places over a beautiful frame-work of gothic structure, astonishing and eliciting remark from passersby.

Besides these, there were all kinds of machinery fluttering and struggling in the air on long poles. Flutter mills and gunboats could be seen making their hasty rounds; men wrestling and turning many kinds of machinery could be taken in at the same glance of the eye. Each regiment had a meeting house and bowers, weather-boarded and covered with pine and cedar boughs, presenting the very picture of enjoyment.

This was the handsomest camp in the whole army, and drawings of it appeared in Harper's Weekly and Frank Leslie, as model camps. It was here the brigade enjoyed soldiering more than at any other time or place before or after, having learned to make its profession agreeable, and looking more particularly to its comfort and enjoyment. Then, there was added to the pleasures of this camp the noted springs, known as Crawfish Springs. A huge stream of bright clear water forces itself from the foot of the hill from whence it issues. They are a natural wonder, and have called forth the admiration of all who chanced to visit them. The slaveocracy of this portion of the South made them their constant summer resort, and the soldiers also enjoyed them as a pleasant retreat to drive dull time away.

The 3rd brigade remained at Lee and Gordon's Mills two months wanting three days, during which time it contracted many fond attachments, and in after times the boys would revert to the memories of this camp with more than ordinary pleasure. It was while here that

Colonel Magee came from Camp McAfee to bid the boys of his regiment good bye, having been unable to leave that place with his command. The colonel's health for a long time had been very poor, and Surgeon Hooton assured him that he could not survive the service, nor do justice to himself and his command by continuing in it.

For these reasons he was induced to offer the resignation of his command, which in due course of time was accepted. There was a universal feeling of sad regret with the boys of the Eighty-sixth at this event, a regret that their beloved colonel no longer had the strength of body to remain with them through the trying events of the future, as he had been their pride through those of the past.

Lieutenant-Colonel D. W. Magee was a man of humane and tender feeling. Having himself served in the ranks in the Mexican War, he was well qualified to appreciate the hardships and difficulties incident to a soldier's life. He was free to converse and associate with his men, at the same time commanding their highest esteem and most submissive obedience. With his gayest humour there mingled a settled air of resolution, which made those who approached him feel they must obey, and which infused love and confidence in those with whom he was surrounded. His manners ingenuous and open-hearted, concealed an imperturbable and calculating spirit. His dress—neither gaudy nor striking, but neat—was such as to set off his person to advantage.

The colonel took his departure from the regiment on Sunday, the 27th of March, with the consciousness of taking with him the hearty "God bless you" of all his men.

Immediately after the resignation of Colonel Magee, the regimental and company officers held an election, and unanimously voted Major Allen L. Fahnestock Colonel of the regiment, who received his commission and was mustered in as such on the 13th of April, 1864, by Captain Cole, of the 9th Indiana. Colonel Fahnestock entered upon the duties of his office with a spirit and resolution that characterized him through all the future events of the regimental history, worthy in every respect the honours of the position left vacant by his energetic predecessor.

At the same time that Colonel Fahnestock was promoted, Captain J. F. Thomas, of Company C, was voted to the position of Major of the regiment.

Major Thomas was a man of a kind and affable disposition, easy and dignified in his intercourse with others, and the real exemplification of the right man in the right place.

CHAPTER 5

Campaign Against Atlanta

Early on the morning of the 3rd of May, 1864, the Third Brigade of the Second Division, Fourteenth Army Corps, under command of Colonel Dan. McCook, left Lee and Gordon's Mills and arrived in Ringgold, a distance of twelve miles, in the afternoon of the same day, and there joined the other two brigades of the division. There was a large army camped in the vicinity of Ringgold, and the hills and valleys were covered with camps, and rung merrily with the voices of many soldiers. It now became evident that the indomitable Sherman was assembling his whole force to make a crushing effort to drive back the threatening rebels under Jo. Johnston.

The few days we remained at Ringgold our army was continually augmenting, when by the 7th of the month it had assembled in force, and set in motion against the enemy at Tunnel Hill and Dalton.

The grand army of the Mississippi, under the immediate command of Major-General Sherman, at the commencement of this campaign, numbered ninety-eight thousand seven hundred and ninety-seven effective men, and two hundred and fifty-four pieces of artillery, and was divided as follows:

The Army of the Cumberland, Major-General Thomas commanding—infantry, fifty-four thousand five hundred and sixty-eight; artillery, two thousand three hundred and seventy-seven; cavalry, three thousand eight hundred and twenty-eight. Total, sixty thousand seven hundred and seventy-three; with one hundred and thirty guns.

Army of the Tennessee, Major-General McPherson commanding—infantry, twenty-two thousand four hundred and thirty-seven; artillery, one thousand four hundred and four; cavalry, six hundred and twenty-four. Total, twenty-four thousand four hundred and sixty-five; with ninety-six guns.

Army of the Ohio, Major-General Schofield commanding—infantry, eleven thousand one hundred and eighty-three; artillery, six hundred and seventy-nine; cavalry, one thousand six hundred and ninety-seven. Total, thirteen thousand five hundred and fifty-nine; with twenty-eight guns.

These numbers continued relatively the same during the campaign, the losses in battle and from sickness being about compensated by recruits, and returns from furlough and hospitals.

The Fourteenth Corps, to which our division belonged, was commanded by Major-General Palmer, and was assigned to a position under Thomas in the centre.

In the move of the grand army on the 7th, our division reached Tunnel Hill at noon, where the enemy made a slight resistance, and while it was getting into position, a battery played upon it from an eminence near the village. This battery was soon dislodged and the enemy put to flight, retreating behind Rocky Face Ridge, where he took up position in Buzzard's Roost Gap, our forces following up rapidly, confronting his position, and throwing up works in case of an attack. The night of the 7th passed off with some skirmish firing in the gap at the Roost, and the next day, nothing was done, only the division changed its front.

The command now held this front until the 12th, during which time there were various demonstrations made on the rebel's invincible position, to no advantage. While here, the Eighty-sixth was continually exposed to the fire of the enemy's sharpshooters, who occupied a position on the highest and most abrupt portions of the Rocky Face Ridge, from whence they viewed us, on the far-spread plain below, as mere Lilliputians of a vile Yankee descent, and shooting among us, often did much injury.

The regiment went on the skirmish line on the afternoon of the 10th, where it spent a most disagreeable night, not being allowed to pitch its tents. An almost continuous skirmish fire was kept up on the 11th, resulting in no very serious casualties to the Eighty-sixth, though the Fifty-second Ohio was made to suffer severely. On the evening of the 11th, our command was relieved by General Cruft's division of the Fourth Army Corps.

In this vicinity was passed a dolesome time, the country being wild and rugged, affording handsome scenery under different circumstances, but for us it had no enchantment. It was at this same gap we fought the enemy on the 25th of February of the same year. Companies H and K had each a man wounded at this place, being the only loss of the regiment.

On the morning of the 12th of May, the Fourteenth Corps, including our division, marched to the right along Rocky Face Ridge, until it came to Snake Creek Gap, and passing through it with much difficulty at a late hour at night, camped on the south-east side of the ridge. Previous to this, General McPherson had taken possession of this gap, completely surprising a brigade of Confederate cavalry which was coming to watch and hold it.

McPherson's and Hooker's commands had gone through before us, and Schofield's followed after us, the Fourth Corps having been left to attract the enemy's attention in front. Thus, the whole army, except Howard's Fourth Corps, moved through Snake Creek Gap, on Resaca. Major-General Thomas took up position on the left of the line, and McPherson and Schofield on his right, the enemy being completely flanked by this move, from his strong position at Buzzard's Roost and Dalton, and compelled to fall back on Resaca. At this place, they determined to give our forces a check, if possible, which moved on their position on the 13th.

On the next day, the 14th, there was hard fighting, our division taking a position late in the afternoon, and building breastworks, the roar of artillery and musketry continuing furiously all the day.

At dusk, on the evening of the 15th, the Eighty-sixth was sent on the skirmish line only a short distance from the rebel works. The enemy was very conversant on this occasion, as was usually the case when their forces took up the retreat, our boys telling them that they would wager their last red that they would be gone before morning; and sure enough, when morning came, every word of this prophecy was verified.

Our commanders, suspecting the action of the rebels, ordered our batteries to play freely on their works. These batteries were stationed on the hills behind the regiment, the screaming missiles from them passing over it, presenting, in the darkness of night, a scene of magnificent grandeur.

In the morning, the rebels had evacuated their works, falling back for a better position, which they never found. In this battle, the regiment lost five, in all; the company loss being as follows: Company C, three wounded; Company H, one wounded, and Company I, one missing. No sooner had the rebels evacuated Resaca than our skirmishers were aware of the fact, so that, by daylight on the 16th, we were in possession of their works, the pursuit being taken up at an early hour.

On the evacuation of Resaca, the Third Brigade passed through it; thence, going back nearly to Snake Creek Gap, and from that place the division continuing along the west side of the Oostanaula river in the direction of Rome, arrived in the vicinity on the 17th, where it met and fought the enemy. The Eighty-sixth Illinois and Twenty-second Indiana were the only regiments generally engaged. These two regiments advancing on the left of the line over uneven and wooded ground, found the enemy and attacked him, a sharp fight ensuing of about twenty minutes in which the foe was worsted, falling back into his intrenchments; and our troops, holding the ground, built rail breastworks. The next morning the rebels were gone, burning the bridge over the Oostanaula after them.

The loss of the Eighty-sixth in this battle, was, five killed and twelve wounded, the company loss being as follows:

Killed.		Wounded	
Company F	2	Company A	3
Company D	1	Company H	1
Company I	1	Company D	4
Company E	1	Company F	2
	—	Company I	2
Total	5		—
		Total	12

On the morning of the 18th, the Eighty-fifth Illinois crossed the river and took possession of the village of Rome, the remainder of the brigade following over in the evening, having to wait for the construction of a rickety pontoon. The people were very much frightened at the event of our entering their village, having formed the idea that the Yankees would extend them no mercy. They told us that they had heard much of Yankee inhumanity, and death was the most clement act they had expected—thus wagged the world with them.

In the possession of Rome, General Jeff. C. Davis' division met with the most gratifying success, capturing its forts, with eight or ten heavy guns, valuable mills, foundries, and various railroad communications. Our brigade remained in Rome six days, the other two brigades of the division not yet having crossed the Oostanaula. During this time, Sherman had halted his whole army along the north side of the Etowah River, in order to rest his troops and complete communications as far as Kingston. This being accomplished, he supplied his wagons with twenty days' rations, and again set his army in motion toward Dallas, nearly south from Kingston, and fifteen miles west from Marietta.

On the 24th day of May, General Davis' command took up the line of march from Rome, crossing the Oostanaula near its mouth, and marching in a southerly direction about twenty miles, camped in a heavy rain storm, the Sixteenth Corps passing it during the night. The next day the division made a forced march over rough and disagreeable roads without gaining much distance, when, late in the evening, distant cannonading could be heard at Dallas. On the 26th the command advanced a short distance beyond Dallas, and drawing up in battle line, built log breastworks, as the Confederate army was lying entrenched in a strong position near this place.

Our lines were advanced still further on the 27th, throwing them into a gap, far in advance of the main line of the battle, and built breastworks, with the appearance of staying awhile.

The enemy about this time made repeated charges on our lines, both to the right and left of us, and several on the lines of the First Brigade, but only one on the Third Brigade. These charges proved very disastrous to the enemy.

The command remained in this position nearly six days without rest, being compelled to lie on its arms, not knowing what moment the enemy might come. This detour of the whole army from the Etowah in its circuit to the right, on Dallas, was made for the purpose of turning Altoona Pass which the rebels determined to hold at all hazards, and proved eminently successful.

On the first of June, our forces began their move from Dallas to the left, in order to contract the lines, and the next position of our division was eight miles to the left of its former one, and still on the left of the Fourth Corps, remaining there two days, skirmishing continually with the enemy until it was relieved and marched further to the left, joining its corps, the Fourteenth; they having been separated since Resaca. Here the boys received a mail, the first for a long while. The corps remained in its position here one day after our division joined it, the enemy evacuating his works on the night of the 5th of June, having been flanked therefrom.

Our forces followed a short distance on the morning of the 6th, but before night took up position, and camped near Ackworth, on the railroad, until the 9th, when they were again set on the move.

After its advance from Ackworth, our army was not long in finding the rebels in another entrenched position.

About this time, General Blair arrived at Ackworth, with two divisions of the Seventeenth Corps and a brigade of cavalry—a reinforcement that amply compensated for our losses in battle, and troops left in garrison at Resaca, Rome, Kingston and Altoona.

On the morning of the 9th, the entire army moved forward to Big Shanty, the next station on the railroad. Here, we found ourselves surrounded by scenery of peculiar and lofty beauty. To our left, and on the east of the railroad, were Sweet Mountain and Black Jack, while to the westward, and nearly in front, rose the bold and striking Kenesaw. To the right was Pine mountain, and more distinctly to the right was Lost mountain.

Here we found the rebel General Johnston, strongly fortified on the northern slopes of Pine, Kenesaw and Lost mountains. General Sherman says, in his official report: "The scene was enchanting; too beautiful to be disturbed by the harsh clamours of war; but the Chattahouchie lay beyond, and I had to reach it."

At this place, our division took a position at right angles with the railroad and a few miles south of Big Shanty, where it threw up substantial breastworks, and remained until the 14th, when the lines were advanced and another line of works thrown up. In front of these works there was a deal of skirmishing carried on, creating undue excitement in the lines of battle, for it was thought the Johnnies would make a trial on our strength and position.

About this time there was an incessant roar of artillery on the extreme right of our lines, despite the heavy rains that fell, which afterwards proved to be the operations of Sherman's "flanking machine."

On Saturday, the 18th, our lines were again moved forward and other works constructed, the boys working with a vengeance all night to find the Johnnies gone in the morning; being flanked and obliged to evacuate their position for another. They were followed up at early dawn on the morning of the 19th, and chased to their next place of retreat. Their right was now found resting on the Marietta and Canton road, with their centre on Kenesaw mountain, and left, across the Lost mountain and Marietta road, behind Nose's creek, and covering the railroad back to the Chattahoochie. Our division under Davis, took its position directly in front of the Big Kenesaw and nearly up to its base.

Several batteries of our artillery soon moved up in short range of the Kenesaw and opened a furious fire upon it, in order, if possible, to develop the whereabouts of the enemy's masked batteries. During this cannonade it seemed that the very heavens were in agitation and the earth in violent commotion, but no reply was received.

The troops stood from behind their works in full view of the enemy, looking on in silent amazement, enjoying in their hearts the sublime grandeur of the scene. Finally, a locomotive was run up to the base of the mountain, when behold, a masked battery opened on it in all its fury, the engine immediately reversing its steam and running back.

On the night of the 20th and 21st, the rebels constructed several strong forts on the summit of the Kenesaw, from whence they annoyed our position a great deal. On the 22nd and 23rd, interesting duels were fought between these batteries of the enemy and our own; and certainly there never was a more amusing and interesting scene portrayed than exhibited in these short, effective engagements.

The scenes about Kenesaw will ever maintain a sacred spot on the tablets of our memory. During operations about this place it rained almost continually for three weeks, so that a general move was impossible.

On the evening of the 25th of June our division was relieved from its position in front of Kenesaw by a division of the 15th Corps, and after much delay arrived at General Palmer's headquarters on the right centre of the army.

The next day Sunday the 26th, it lay in the rear of the lines of battle, resting itself for the dreadful scenes of the morrow. The loss of the Eighty-sixth Regiment, from Dallas up to this time, was nine wounded and one killed; the company loss was as follows:

Company I, one killed.

Wounded	
Company A	1
Company I	1
Company E	1
Company F	1
Company D	2
Company K	1
Company B	2
Total	9

On the 24th of June, General Sherman ordered that two assaults should be made on the 27th, one by General McPherson's troops near Little Kenesaw, and another by General Thomas', about one mile further south. This came wholly unexpected to his troops, all believing that he would put "the flanking machine" in force whenever he made a demonstration on the enemy's position, but Sherman resolved to execute any plan that promised success. These two assaults were made at the time and manner prescribed in the order, and both failed.

General Thomas chose the 2nd division of the 14th Corps to aid in the work along his line, and early on the morning of the 27th it was massed preparatory to a charge. The 3rd brigade, Colonel Dan. McCook commanding, was on the left of the division; the 2nd brigade, Colonel Mitchell commanding, was on the right, and the 1st brigade, General Morgan commanding, was held in the rear as reserves. The signal for the charge was given at 8 a.m., by the simultaneous discharge of a battery of guns; the lines advancing slow and steady, passing over our line of works, descending a hill over a small stream, then crossing an open field, ascended the acclivity on which the enemy's works were built, when a desperate rush was made upon them with all the fortitude and heroism of men under a most galling fire of cannon and musketry.

The brigade on our right failing to come up, we had to receive the cross-fire of the enemy. It was too withering, the men falling before it as the grass before the scythe. When the works were reached by those who did not fall in the attack, they were too weak and too few in number to effect a breach in them, the men lying down in front of the works and up against them, until the order to fall back was given. When the order of retreat was given, it was hard to obey, being attended with a greater slaughter than the assault, the enemy having the chance of taking cool and deliberate aim. Thus our broken lines fell back, again taking position only thirty yards from the enemy, and in the most difficult manner threw up a line of works, at the same time hugging the ground for dear life, and where we remained in defiance of the exultant rebels. This was our darkest day of the war.

The loss of the brigade on this occasion was truly severe. Colonel Daniel McCook fell mortally wounded, and Colonel Harmon succeeding him, survived his command but one moment, when he was carried off the field a corpse.

The total loss of the regiment in this charge, in killed, wounded and missing, was ninety-six men.

The company loss was as follows:

Killed.

Company A	11
Company C	4
Company D	2
Company F	3
Company G	2
Company H	2
Company I	3
Company K	1
Loss in killed	28

Wounded.

Company A	7
Company B	3
Company C	6
Company D	9
Company E	5
Company G	7
Company H	13
Company K	5
Loss in wounded	55

Missing.

Company A	6
Company D	2
Company F	1
Loss in missing	9
Officers wounded	4

Ninety-six men were lost from the Eighty-sixth on that fatal day. It was a loss to be remembered and remarked, for they were among our foremost and best men. They were as noble, as true and trusty men, as loving and as loyal as ever lived.

May a just Heaven reward them as their merit deserves! May the earth rest light on their bones! Mourn them not; it was with them *dulce et decorum, est pro patria mori.* How well these men have fought and with what heroism they have suffered, let the battles of Chick-amauga, Mission Ridge and Kenesaw answer! They will be rewarded, for they have left their "footprints on the sands of time."

It was now a busy time at the hospitals, for they were full of the most heart-rending cases. Among the physicians conspicuous there for energy and ability, were the indefatigable Hooton and Guth—men who justly deserved the confidence and respect of their boys. Among the most trying positions in the army, the Surgeon's is first. The minds and dispositions of soldiers are as varied as the colours of the kaleido-scope, and hard to comprehend even in a sound condition, but when fretted by ill health no one man could come out best with all of them. A good Surgeon, like the whimsical pages of Tristram Shandy, is pes-tily censured and admired alternately.

The 3rd brigade held its position in close proximity to the enemy's works for six days, until the 3rd of July. It was a hard one indeed, for we were obliged to hug the works and keep concealed all the time, night and day. Bullets were continually buzzing round in threatening and unfriendly style. An interesting incident occurred, however, on the 29th, that broke the monotony of our situation for a short time; it was an armistice of a few hours to bury our dead, the stench hav-ing become so offensive to both parties that it could be no longer endured.

Details were sent from every company to perform the last office to the heroic dead. This having been done, and a headboard erected with the name of each upon it, to mark the spot where rests the sleep-ing brave, the armistice was concluded. Soon after the armistice our brigade, now under command of Colonel Dillworth, began a trench with the intention of undermining the enemy's works, and blowing them up, but suspecting something underhanded on our part, they threw turpentine balls between the lines, which would certainly have disclosed any outward movement, but the movement was inward, and their handsome fires availed them nothing.

This experiment, however, was followed by another, more suc-cessful. By placing a drum on the solid ground and a marble on the head of it, they discovered a jar in the earth. This was sufficient, and gathering up their traps they evacuated early in the evening of the 2nd of July, our forces following on the morning of the 3rd. If the rebels had not evacuated when they did, the 3rd brigade would have had a grand jubilee on the 4th, for by that time it would have succeeded in laying a magazine under their works, and setting it off would have raised their ideas.

On the evening of the 3rd of July, our forces again came upon

Johnston's army entrenched at Smyrna Church, five miles from Marietta, and forming our lines so as to confront his position, lay here until after the 4th.

On the morning of the 5th, Johnston had fallen back to another line of entrenchments on the north side of the Chattahoochie, our lines advancing as usual until they came upon him. We were now in sight of the Gate City, its steeples and spires appearing in the distance. For the first time we beheld the object of our toils and marches, every heart rejoicing to behold the doomed Atlanta. General Sherman was not content, however, until every vestige of the Confederate army was upon the south side of the Chattahoochie. Accordingly, he ordered his "flanking machine," under command of General Schofield, to cross the river and operate on the enemy's flank.

General Schofield crossed the Chattahoochie on the 7th of July, compelling an evacuation of the enemy's works on the 9th, their whole force crossing to the Atlanta side of the river and burning the bridge after them; and thus, on the morning of the 10th, Sherman's army held undisputed possession of the right bank of the Chattahoochie; one of the chief objects of his campaign was gained, and Atlanta lay before him only eight miles distant. It was too important a place in the hands of the enemy to be left undisturbed, with its magazines, stores, arsenals, workshops, foundries and converging railways.

But the army had worked hard and needed rest. Therefore it was put in camp in favourable positions along the Chattahoochie, General Davis' division of Palmer's corps camping near the railroad and wagon bridge across the river. While we were encamped at this place, the adventuresome boys would go near the banks of the river and gather blackberries, notwithstanding the continuous fire of the rebel pickets on the opposite side, there being scarcely a soldier who would not risk his life for a blackberry.

The 3rd brigade remained in this camp just eight days, when on the 18th, it crossed the Chattahoochie river at Paice's ferry several miles above our camp, the other two brigades having preceded it on the same route.

After crossing the river, the division advanced cautiously in line of battle, preparatory for any emergency. The advance was made over woody and uneven ground, although not to say very broken. Shortly before night, the command took up a position on favourable ground, the front lines building rail breastworks. During the night, there was some skirmish firing in our immediate front, though it was not sufficient to prevent the boys from gathering blackberries, which had to be had, Johnnies or no Johnnies.

On the morning of the 19th, at ten o'clock a.m., the division was again put on the move, going further to the right and front. It halted a short time at Peach Tree Creek until a crossing could be made over it. The Eighty-sixth and One Hundred and Twenty-fifth Illinois were the last of the 3rd brigade to cross over this creek, the other regiments having made the passage and engaged the enemy in battle beyond the crest of the hills bordering on this stream, finding them almost an overmatch. At this juncture, Colonel Fahnestock was ordered to hasten his regiment to their assistance, for the left of the line was giving ground.

In obedience to orders, the Eighty-sixth crossed the creek on a foot log, being greatly scattered by the time all were across. The scattered regiment formed at the foot of the hills on which our skirmishers were engaging the rebels, and then advanced to their support. Having taken up position, and thrown up a light line of works, the rebels in superior force charged on our skirmishers, driving them back pell-mell on the main line, which, after a desperate struggle, repulsed them with heavy loss. The enemy in this charge came near flanking the Eighty-sixth out of its position, the right giving back a short distance at first, but soon resumed it again. Despite the disadvantage in numbers, in this spirited engagement, our forces maintained their own, and when night came, good earthworks were thrown up in readiness for any emergency.

The loss of the brigade in this battle was almost as great as was sustained in the charge on Kenesaw; the regiments on the skirmish line being all cut to pieces, and half their number killed and captured. Many a lifeless form was left unheralded on the field of battle, and the evening shades of the ever memorable 19th of July drew her mantle of darkness over a field of blood.

The loss of the Eighty-sixth, in this battle, was comparatively light, being ten in all.

The company loss was as follows:

	Killed.
Company D	2
Company B	1
Company H	1
Total	4

49

	Wounded.
Company B	1
Company D	2
Company C	1
Company F	1
Company I	1
	—
Total	6

The next morning after the battle, at daylight, a rebel line of works could be seen about four hundred yards in our front. There was nothing in them, however, but a small skirmish force, the main body having withdrawn. The Eighty-sixth kept up a heavy skirmish fire on these works, not allowing a Johnny-reb to show his head except he got a volley of musketry. Four pieces of artillery were brought on the line and opened on these works, having great effect and causing them to be evacuated. When a rebel would turn his back to run, half a regiment would salute him, in its modest way. This was fun for the boys and they seemed to relish it.

On the 21st, a reconnoitering expedition was sent out to ascertain the strength and whereabouts of the enemy, and after advancing one mile and a half found him in force, strongly intrenched, and then returned.

There being now nothing to confront it, our division moved forward on the 22nd, and passing a line of intrenchments which were found evacuated, arrived and camped within three or four miles of Atlanta—the Gate City of the South. In this position, our brigade was left in reserve, the first time on the whole campaign, having, however, to keep a regiment on a hill, half a mile in advance of the main line of works, as a lookout. While on this eminence, the boys had some sociable times with the Johnnies, trading and exchanging with them as long as agreeable, there being an agreement that there should be no shooting while trafficking was going on.

On the 22nd, the day on which General McPherson was killed, there was hard fighting on the left, Hood having massed his forces in the hope to crush it, but after the most desperate fighting of the campaign, his efforts were foiled, and he was compelled to withdraw with an overwhelming loss. Sherman's report of a few days after, gave the enemy's loss as six to our one.

The Second Division of the Fourteenth Corps was moved from its position on the morning of the 28th, and marched to the right. It was now that General James D. Morgan took command of it, General Davis being indisposed. General Morgan was ordered to move his command by Turner's Ferry and East Point and come in on the flank of General Howard's new line, so that, in case of an attack it would catch the attacking rebel force in flank or rear.

This plan proved abortive by the sickness of General Davis and mistake of roads by General Morgan, who, by this mishap was greatly delayed. Meantime, Hardee and Lee sallied forth from Atlanta by the Bell's Ferry road, and formed their masses in the open fields behind a swell of ground, and after some heavy artillery firing, advanced in parallel lines against the Fifteenth Corps, expecting to catch it in air; but Sherman was prepared for this very contingency; our troops were expecting this attack and met it with a raking fire of musketry, which thinning the ranks of the enemy, compelled him to withdraw in confusion. After this, at some points, six or seven successive efforts were made to carry our works, but all of them proved futile.

Had our division not been delayed by causes beyond control, what was simply a complete repulse of the enemy would have been a disastrous rout. The rebel slain in this day's fight was enormous. Dead men never lay in greater numbers on the same sized piece of ground. Our men buried 2,840, exclusive of those carried off by their own men.

Late in the evening of the 28th, or rather, early on the morning of the 29th, after a most fatiguing tramp, our division reached the main line. In the afternoon of the 29th, the division advanced the lines of battle and took position; and again, on the 30th, it moved to the right and advancing the lines took up position. On the 31st, it left its works and marched still further to the right, on a reconnoissance, returning to its works the same day. On this reconnoissance we got a fine ducking, having left our rubbers in camp.

On the 4th of August, the division was again moved to the right, and advancing the lines at least one mile, after several halts, built works under a severe cannonade from the enemy's batteries. After some hard skirmishing and changing about, the 3rd Division of the 14th Corps relieved General Morgan's command; it moved further to the right and front, on the 12th, relieving a command of raw troops of the 23rd Corps.

Here we found breastworks and were not constrained to labour as much as usual on such occasions. The command remained in this last position without any unusual occurrences only the spirited bombardment of the city of Atlanta by our batteries of heavy guns, being kept up at regular intervals night and day. The skirmish firing was also kept up with animation on both sides and along the entire lines. Now and then the monotony was broken by a conversation or trade, but never to last a great while, the foe not allowing their men such liberties when it could be helped, for they would not unfrequently take advantage of these occasions to desert.

However, on the 19th of August, our brigade was marched several miles to the right, in support of the 23rd Corps, as it was thought the enemy would charge its lines on that occasion, but the supposition did not prove a reality. The brigade returned the same day without adventure to its former camp. Then again, on the succeeding day, the division was moved off in the same direction of the day previous, but not stopping so soon as before. This time, we passed the right wing of the army entirely, and bearing south-east struck the Atlanta and Montgomery railroad not far distant from East Point. After injuring the railroad all that lay in its power, the division returned to camp, having enjoyed a drenching rain. Nothing more of interest passed off except the hum-drum picket firing, until the siege of the doomed Atlanta was raised.

It was on the memorable 27th of August, that Sherman's entire force was withdrawn from about the beleaguered city, and the whole of it, except the 20th Army Corps, which moved to the fortifications at the railroad on the Chattahoochie, marched in the direction of the Macon railway for the purpose of severing the enemy's communications. Early on the morning of the 27th, all the troops on the left of our division having changed front the day previous, it moved from the breastworks, and during the day took its position on the new line.

On the evening of this same day, the Eighty-sixth regiment held its second anniversary. It had been the intention had not the movement of the army interfered, to appropriate a part of the day for this purpose, but as the regiment was on the move all day it was under the necessity of taking the night.

Accordingly, in the evening, the men were assembled on the colour line and the objects of the meeting announced. A committee of three: Major Thomas, Captains Bogardus and French, were appointed to draft resolutions.

The committee having retired, Chaplain Millsaps made a speech appropriate to the occasion, when the resolutions were called for and read. They were strong in favor of the administration and bitter against the copperheads. Though the regiment was not permitted to vote, it could, nevertheless, express its sentiments to its friends, and in behalf of the country. These resolutions were unanimously adopted, there being no dissenting voice, and ordered to be sent to the Chicago Tribune, Peoria Transcript and Peoria Mail. Speeches were then made by Surgeon Hooton, Colonel Dillworth, Major Thomas, Captain Bogardus and others, of a stirring and patriotic nature. This anniversary was, under the circumstances, highly interesting indeed, and all the surviving members who were there, will be duly wont to review it with feelings of pride.

When Sherman's army had withdrawn from the siege of Atlanta, the enemy supposed he had taken up his line of retreat and abandoned the enterprise. While in this belief, they were destined to have a jubilant time; and to make it the merrier still, a mandate was sent out to the country about for all to come and partake of the fatted calf. Fair damsels flocked from the vicinity about to partake in the joy over victory; but lo! in the meantime, the Yankees cut the Macon railroad so that the birdies from the rural districts could not get to their homes, and aged mothers cried in vain for their affectionate daughters, wishing the Yankees many a curse for interfering in their jubilee.

Ah! their day of rejoicing had too soon turned to one of tears, their unhappy city had been relieved from a siege only to be captured. O, the bitter disappointments that overtake short-sighted man! One hour he rejoices, the next he mourns! How varied the fortunes of war; today the city is impenetrable, tomorrow it has fallen! Poor, proud Atlanta revelled, rejoiced and wept the same day!

After the siege of Atlanta was abandoned it was not long until our division, under General J. D. Morgan, arrived in the vicinity of Jonesboro, about twenty-two miles south of Atlanta. At this place, on the 1st of September, and at five o'clock p.m., our division was formed for a charge: the 2nd brigade on the right, the 3rd brigade in the centre, and the 1st brigade on the left, and advanced to the attack in two lines of battle. The Eighty-sixth regiment in this battle held a position in the second line. The enemy's works were handsomely carried, capturing a greater part of rebel General Gowan's brigade, including its commander, with two four-gun batteries. This brigade was among the choice men of the rebel army, having fought with a desperation worthy a better cause.

This charge came like a flash upon the enemy, who were not aware of our coming until we pounced upon them like an avalanche, and though they fought obstinately, they were completely conquered.

Our brigade was in the hottest of the fight, and among the first troops to scale the works and capture them.

The loss of the Eighty-sixth Regiment in this battle was two killed and sixteen wounded. The company loss was as follows:

	Killed.
Company F	1
Company I	1
Total	2

	Wounded.
Company A	1
Company B	1
Company D	2
Company G	4
Company I	1
Company H	5
Company E	1
Company K	1
Total	16

The night after the battle of Jonesboro an explosion of a tremendous character was heard in the direction of Atlanta, for the enemy were evacuating it and burning their magazines.

The disheartened and disorganized forces of the enemy now exerted all their energies to complete a successful withdrawal, and save themselves from utter annihilation. One wing of Hood's army fled precipitately down the Macon railroad, and the other retreated along the Augusta road.

Thus was Atlanta evacuated on the night of the 1st of September, after so long a period of time. Remaining a few days in the vicinity of Jonesboro, the 3rd brigade was put in charge of the prisoners and sent with them to Atlanta on the 4th. It kept a jealous eye to its charge, conducting them to the desired place with undue rapidity. The day was hot and water scarce. Many of the boys under their heavy loads gave out and laid down to rest. Rebel and Yank laid down together, and as best they could followed up after they had become rested.

The blame of this unmasterly march was laid to Colonel Langley, who was then in command of the brigade, Colonel Dillworth having been wounded in the late battle. When the command arrived in

Atlanta, not more than one-half the men were with it, being left tired and worn out along the wayside. Many of the prisoners might have made their escape, for all were huddled and mixed up in all manner of ways.

There was much sympathy expressed by the citizens of Atlanta towards these prisoners as they were marched and counter-marched through several of the principal streets of the city. Weeping and moaning and lamentation was the principal order of the occasion. The prisoners were finally put in the "bull-pen," and the brigade permitted to go into camp. We were now in the great city for the first time, that place for which we had so long fought and laboured to possess. It had been much impaired by the bombardment, the effects of our heavy guns being discernible in various parts.

Thus ended the great campaign against Atlanta—the Gate City of the South—after one hundred and twenty days of the most trying scenes through which an army ever passed. During this time we were under the almost continual fire of the enemy, amounting to little else than an incessant battle. The Eighty-sixth Regiment was in eight regular engagements of the most desperate and trying nature. Our dear comrades were daily falling around us and by us, but still we pressed on and finished the work in which they were so ardently enlisted.

At the fall of Atlanta the hopes of the nation revived and the cause of the Union was materially aided. The great anaconda of secession was palsied and made to fade! A new-born nation rejoiced in the beginning dawn of peace and liberty! The heart of a free, loyal people was made to leap for joy!

There were many thrilling and exciting incidents connected with this campaign, among which we will narrate the one respecting Captain Jo. Major. In the charge on Kenesaw, on the 27th of June, while only a few feet from the enemy's works, Captain Major was struck in the breast with a stone thrown by a rebel, which knocked him senseless for a time, and during this state the lines had fallen back, leaving him alone among the dead and dying. Regaining himself, by and by he ascertained his condition, but determining not to be a prisoner, he resolved to play the dying man. He lay, therefore, in a seemingly helpless state, closing his eyes and gasping as if the next breath was to be his last. Finally, a rebel came to where he lay, and took his sword and other valuables.

The dying man made signs for water, and the rebel held a canteen to his mouth, but, poor man! he could not drink. After this, other rebels from their works shot at him, but he did not budge, and believing him really in the throes of death, they did not bother him anymore. The day was extremely hot; it was one of those warm summer days peculiar to the South. He lay on his back in the burning sun—an impossible thing under other circumstances. Flies and ants swarmed his face, and bit and stung him, but he dared not move.

He was kept in this position from 9 o'clock a.m. until after dark; but night coming on, he took leg-bail for our works, reaching them without further adventure. He came to his company hatless, swordless, moneyless, but sound as ever—the same old Jo.

CHAPTER 6

To the Rear

The casualties of the Eighty-sixth Regiment, on the long and arduous campaign against Atlanta, was one hundred and seventy-nine men in killed, wounded and missing.

Besides this number, there were many who were taken sick and sent back to hospitals. Thus, when the campaign had ended, the regiment was materially reduced in numbers. It was now not much larger than two full companies; and then, the companies themselves were mere skeletons, some of them not exceeding a corporal's squad. These were certainly trying times with the soldiers, being attended with constant hardships, privations and adventures, from the beginning of the campaign to its end. But still, those who did pass the fiery ordeal, stood up to it like men, with fine spirits and light hearts, doing all that men could do.

After some changing about, the brigade took up permanent quarters in the outskirts of the city on the south-west side near the railroad. The regiment now fixed up its camp in a substantial manner, and for a long time took the military world easy, spending most of its time in going to and from the city in pursuit of pleasure, and such.

There was not a little trading going on about this time with those who had a disposition that way; in fact, it seemed that Sherman's whole army had been suddenly metamorphosed into tobacco traders and other kinds of merchants.

Atlanta was overstocked with tobacco, held by private individuals, which was bought by the soldiers at low rates and peddled out with handsome profits. Thus passed the time right briskly, all seeming to have forgotten the past and to be living for the present only.

Shortly after the occupation of Atlanta, General Sherman ordered all non-combatants to leave the city, going north or south as their inclinations and interests might lead them. This order fell on the ears of the inhabitants of Atlanta like a thunderbolt. Though they had lent all the moral and physical assistance in their power to the cause of the rebellion, they had begun to dream of the advent of the Federal troops as the commencement of an era of quiet. They had never imagined the war would reach Atlanta. Now that it had come, and kept its rough, hot hand upon them for so many days, they were beginning to look forward to a long period when they might enjoy at once the advantages of the protection of a just and powerful government, and the luxuries it would thus afford them. It was indeed a pitiful sight to see these reluctant people leave their homes and property, but such was the necessity in the case that it must be done.

Such are the cruel mandates of war, and they were obliged to abide its consequences, having waged and maintained it.

About the middle of September there was an armistice of some days to provide an exit south for these unfortunate people, and for the exchange of prisoners captured in the last campaign.

General James D. Morgan's division remained in Atlanta at its ease until the 29th of September, when it boarded the cars and was transported, *via* Chattanooga and Huntsville, to near Athens, Alabama. From this place it was sent on an expedition against General Forrest, who had been making demonstrations on our railroads, having destroyed much of the Nashville and Decatur road.

When the division arrived at Athens, Forrest was crossing the Tennessee at Florence, retreating out of our way as fast as possible. With rapid marches General Morgan reached Florence in two days, distant from Athens about forty-five miles. The creeks and rivers on the route were swollen, but he never stopped for them, for wading through, we went plodding on. The division arrived within a few miles of Florence on the evening of the 5th of October, and entered it on the 6th without opposition, the enemy having completed his crossing. The division could follow no further, and on the morning of the 10th began its return march, arriving back in Athens on the 12th, where it boarded the cars on its return to Chattanooga.

The command arrived at Chattanooga in the night of the 14th, and went into camp where there was neither wood nor water. The march from Athens to Florence and back again was, under the circumstances, probably the severest the Eighty-sixth Regiment ever made; at least, it stands among the hardest. The rains fell in torrents, but notwithstanding, the command was rushed headlong on through the mad waters of

58

Flint and Duck rivers, in many places up to the soldier's armpits.

While the division remained in Chattanooga there was a deal of excitement and uncertainty respecting the movements of rebel General Hood, who was making a demonstration on our rear, the command being in readiness to march at a moment's notice.

General Sherman, however, soon changed his course, so that Hood was obliged to take a circuitous route to the west and north. To follow Hood indefinitely, without much prospect of overtaking and overwhelming his army, would be for Sherman equivalent to being decoyed out of Georgia. To remain on the defensive, on the other hand, would be to lose the main effectiveness of his army. Sherman had previously proposed to General Grant to destroy the railway from Atlanta to Chattanooga, and strike out through Georgia.

"By attempting to hold the roads," he wrote, "we will lose a thousand men monthly, and will gain no result."

And again:

"Hood may turn into Tennessee and Kentucky, but I believe he will be forced to follow me. Instead of being on the defensive I would be on the offensive. Instead of guessing at what he means, he would have to guess at my plans. I prefer to march through Georgia, smashing things, to the sea."

And again:

"When you hear I am off, have lookouts at Morris' Island, S.C.; Ossabaw Sound, Georgia; Pensacola and Mobile bays. I will turn up somewhere, and believe me I can take Macon, Milledgeville, Augusta, and Savannah, Georgia, and wind up with closing the neck back of Charleston, so that they will starve out. This movement is not purely military or strategic, but it will illustrate the vulnerability of the South."

General Grant promptly authorized the proposed movement, indicating, however, his preference for Savannah as the objective, and fixing Dalton as the northern limit for the destruction of the railway. Preparations were immediately made for the execution of these plans.

Early on the morning of the 18th, General Morgan marched his division to rejoin the Army of the Cumberland, which at this time lay in reserve at Galesville, Alabama, taking with him a large drove of cattle for army consumption. The division reached the army and joined its corps at 11 a.m. on the 22nd.

Sherman had issued orders for his army to subsist off the country, which it did with a good will, foragers being sent out from the different commands daily. The country round Galesville was wild and romantic, affording that beautiful scenery so peculiar to northern Georgia and Alabama.

The army was soon again put on the move, part of it going with General Thomas, and the remainder, the 14th, 20th, 15th and 17th Corps, going with Sherman down the railway towards Atlanta.

Morgan's division marched to Rome, where it remained a few days, after which it continued on to Kingston, where it arrived on the 1st of November. At Kingston the army received eight months pay, and a partial supply of clothing, having to wait until it arrived at Atlanta before a complete supply would be issued.

While at Kingston, it will be remembered, the Eighty-sixth Regiment camped on a piece of ground covered with all manner of stones, from the minutest pebble to those that were large enough to make an uneven bed. Again, on the 8th of the month, the division marched on, passing through the ruined Cassville on to Cartersville, where it halted a few days, at one time going to guard the railroad, which did not last long enough to make it pay.

Cartersville is noted for the most remarkable of the monumental remains in the United States. They are situated upon the right bank of the Etowah river near the railroad, some two miles south of the town, in the midst of a perfectly level alluvial bottom, towering above all surrounding objects, changeless amid the revolutions of centuries. On good testimony it has been urged that these mounds were built by a race of people preceding the Indian race. Who they were, and how great that population was, cannot now be determined. No historian has left the record of their manners, government and laws; no voice save that silent speaking testimony of these monuments, proclaims their past greatness. No reply is heard in definite response by those who knock at their tombs. The morning the Eighty-sixth left this place, Billy Longfellow issued rations on the summit of one of these mounds, and the regiment stacked arms along the road near them.

On the morning of the 13th, the 2nd division of the 14th Corps was set in motion from Cartersville toward Atlanta, destroying the railway, foundries, mills, etc., on its route. In not a few instances private dwellings and private property were laid desolate. Previous to this, General Sherman had directed all surplus artillery, all baggage not needed for the contemplated march, all the sick and wounded, refugees and other encumbrances, to be sent back to Chattanooga. On its march to Atlanta the division passed over much of the old campaign ground, which had lost none of its familiarity, seeming as if there had been no lapse of time.

The Kenesaw was natural, and the dreadful battlefield of the 27th of June, where so many of our slain comrades lie buried, and whose graves were yet fresh, had undergone no change except that the leaves had ripened and fallen to the ground. Even as the leaves wither and fall, so must man, and we were made sad in contemplating the fearful, bloody past.

The division crossed the Chattahoochie River in the forenoon of the 15th, and arrived in Atlanta in time to draw clothing, provisions, etc., preparatory to the uncertain actions of the morrow. Atlanta on this occasion seemed to be swallowed up in flames. Bright, lurid lights were seen springing up in every quarter. It seemed that the once proud and defiant city was bidding earth farewell! "But what is now to be done?" everyone asks. "Has Sherman gone crazy, sure enough?" Thus people talked, the country over. They could not tell what Sherman was up to now. He moved out from Atlanta on the 16th of November into the darkness and wilderness of Dixie, leaving the good folks at home to wonder where Sherman had gone. But several weeks elapsed before the secret was divulged—before the lost hero rose up in the magic of his might on the great seaboard.

CHAPTER 7

To the Sea

With this chapter begins the narrative of the great raid through Georgia down to the sea. Now was begun a military feat which when accomplished astonished the world, and proved false the maxim laid down by military geniuses of every notoriety and age, that no army could subsist any length of time without a permanent base of supplies. The undertaking of a raid of so great magnitude and daring was an act bearing the tint of insanity and reckless daring beyond the comprehension of learned critics and wire-cutters.

For the purpose of this great march, Sherman had divided his army into two wings; the right commanded by Major General Oliver O. Howard, comprising the 15th and 17th Corps; the left under Major General Henry W. Slocum, comprising the 14th and 20th Corps. The 14th Corps, to which the Eighty-sixth Illinois belonged, was composed of three divisions, led by Brigadier Generals William P. Carlin, James D. Morgan and Absalom Baird. The 3rd brigade of General Morgan's division, to which the Eighty-sixth regiment more immediately belonged, was commanded on this great raid by Colonel Langley, of the 125th Illinois.

About 12 m., on the 16th of November, 1864, General Morgan's command led out from Atlanta along the Augusta and Atlanta railroad, following and destroying it as far as Covington; here the division left it, marching through Shady Dale, near Edenton Factory, directly on to Milledgeville, the capital of the State, where it arrived late in the evening of the 22nd. Our march to the capital of Georgia was one of pleasure and plenty; plenty sat smiling on every hand, tauntingly inviting the Yankee boys on.

The Eighty-sixth was now in the height of its glory, making itself free in every man's potato patch, poultry yard and smoke house, thus assuring the inhabitants of its sincere regard and thankfulness for their unswerving devotion as enemies. Thus the command passed merrily on in its wild paroxysms of frantic joy, living as sumptuously as kings are wont to live in their marble palaces and wanton luxuries. Time did not drag heavily with us, nor did the ghost of hunger haunt us in our dreams. We laid down at night on a bed of pine boughs with as much composure as if feathers had been at our command. We dared famine to look us in the face, and treated discontent with contempt.

The commonest produce of the country so far was sweet potatoes or yams, and negro beans. These vegetables, with all kinds of meat, afforded high living, and in a plentiful manner. The boys were never under the necessity of carrying much provisions with them; in fact, they scarcely ever carried any in these parts, for when the column stopped for meals they would climb the fence for sweet potatoes, and shoot a shoat for meat. About half an hour before the troops went into camp, firing might be heard in every direction about the column, being caused by the boys shooting porkers and such, for their supper.

There was a great caravan of negroes hanging on the rear of our column when it arrived in Milledgeville, like a sable cloud in the sky before a thunder storm or tornado. They thought it was freedom now or never, and would follow whether or no. It was really a ludicrous sight to see them trudging on after the army in promiscuous style and divers manner. Some in buggies of the most costly and glittering manufacture; some on horseback, the horses old and blind, and others on foot; all following up in right jolly mood, bound for the Elysium of ease and freedom.

Let those who choose to curse the negro curse him; but one thing is true, despite the unworthiness they bear on many minds, that they were the only friends on whom we could rely for the sacred truth in the sunny land of Dixie. What they said might be relied on so far as they knew; and one thing more, they knew more and could tell more than most of the poor white population. Milledgeville was occupied by our forces without the slightest opposition on the part of the enemy, there being no enemy of material consequence to contend with, all having gone to Nashville, there to get a complete drubbing.

On the morning of the 24th our division marched through Milledgeville, and passing on through Sandersville, crossed the Ogechee River and Rocky Comfort Creek into Louisville, a county seat town, where it remained several days to let the right wing of the army come up on a line. Milledgeville is beautifully situated in the paradise portion of

Georgia, the country around being rich, and on the whole, level and fertile. The city itself is laid off with much good taste, the streets being wide and handsome, and the buildings sparsely built along them. The private dwellings, for the most part, were framework, not costly and extravagant, but constructed in plain and wholesome style.

The State House, however, was especially grand in its design and material. On leaving this place our forces destroyed many of the public buildings. The Oconee River, which flows along the east side of the capitol, is a narrow, deep stream, and very handsome. Over it was a good wagon bridge, left unhurt by the rebel fugitives. While crossing this bridge all pack animals over one to a company, were taken and appropriated to other use, for by general order only one was allowed to a company, but in spite of orders the boys would cling to their mules, one company having sometimes several span. These creatures were a great help to us in carrying our heavy plunder.

On the march from Milledgeville to Sandersville the command was for the first time molested seriously by the cavalry of the enemy. About these times they captured many of our foragers, nineteen of whom it was said were hung on the spot.

The day on which the command entered Sandersville it had its first encounter with the enemy's cavalry, under rebel General Wheeler, which had gotten in our front and attempted to arrest our progress.

But there was no halting on Wheeler's account, for our troops made their way on, he and his getting out of the way. While the division was at Sandersville it gave the country around a healthy forage. A certain wealthy planter living near had five or six score of French or Spanish negroes, with a dwarfish stature and a gabble like so many geese. This planter lived in Savannah in high life, as most wealthy planters do. His possessions would seem changed when next he saw them; his cotton and out-houses, his presses and gins were burned up, his productions taken and plantation gleaned; but he is not alone in his misery, his neighbours are as bad off as himself.

It was amusing to see the slouchy negroes obey the soldiers' orders, for they had to be obeyed. Twenty or thirty of them would run after the same chicken, heading and tripping each other as they went. These, like all negroes, were delighted to see the Yankees waltz in and make old *massa* "shell out." They would point out where things were concealed, and then! Oh, then! take a regular nigger laugh when the Yanks "went in."

However, about noon on the 28th, the command having left

Sandersville, arrived on the west bank of Rocky Comfort creek. The bridge over this stream being burnt, it was obliged to wait till late in the evening before a crossing could be effected into Louisville, where it went into camp one mile east of the town.

At this camp, on the evening of the 29th, Colonel Fahnestock took his regiment on picket, and on the next day fought a force of the enemy's cavalry which was making a demonstration on our lines in several places, keeping the pickets on the manoeuvre most of the day.

At the first alarm of the enemy on the lines of the Eighty-sixth, the Colonel ordered his men to advance to a line two hundred yards to his front and throw up a line of barricades for protection.

While this was being done a constant fire was kept up on the rebels, whose course was soon turned, being compelled to withdraw in confusion across a large cornfield. When they reached the farther side of this field they formed their lines, and also threw up a line of barricades which they held until late in the afternoon, when the regiment charged them away and took possession, and following them up for more than a mile, returned. Though the casualties of the regiment in this day's skirmish were not great, the excitement, nevertheless, ran high. Its loss was four missing or captured. The company loss was as follows: Co. A, two; Co. F, one; Co. K, one.

The foragers from our division on this occasion were made to suffer severely. The enemy came upon them so suddenly that they were unable to get back to the lines; not a few of them were killed and captured, and many of them, being overbalanced with wines, were shot in cold blood.

On the first of December, the division moved from Louisville in the direction of Millen, and crossing on its route, Big, Dry and Spring Creeks, camped a short distance to the east of the latter. It had the corps train in charge, while the other two divisions moved on the right and left to protect it.

The next day a deflection was made in the line of march of our division, caused by the change of direction of the 20th Corps, its course being turned northward, crossing Buckhead and Rocky Creeks, on pontoons laid for that purpose, and camping on the night of the 3rd at Lumpkin's on the railroad. On the next day Carlin's and Morgan's divisions, with the three corps trains, after destroying three miles of railway, moved in the direction of Jacksonboro, and camped thirteen miles beyond Lumpkin's Station. On this same day, Baird and Kilpatrick, after some fighting with Wheeler's cavalry, drove the enemy from Waynesboro and across Brier creek.

The march was continued on the morning of the 5th, passing through Jacksonboro into the north-eastern edge of Effingham County, thence down the Savannah River, arriving in the vicinity of the city of Savannah on the 11th of December.

Many new and exciting incidents occurred on the march from Louisville to Savannah. Larger caravans of negroes than before followed our war-path, frequently being cut off by the enemy's cavalry, but by circuitous routes and much hard marching, would make their appearance again.

There was at once a laughable and pitiful sight occurred respecting these poor unfortunates, while the command was crossing the country in the vicinity of Buckhead and Rocky Creeks. As soon as the troops crossed these streams the pontoons were taken up and the Africans left behind. This, however, did not have the effect to discourage them, for, after wandering up and down the banks for a time, in mad excitement, some sturdy fellow among the rest, ventured in and swam across. This was a signal for the rest, who followed like sheep in a drove. Many of the women, with the darling calamity of their bosom in their arms, were washed under by the swift current to rise no more.

The inhabitants of Georgia, on this unexpected raid through their country, used many devices in the effort to hide their household affairs, horses, mules, wagons and all kinds of provisions from the invading Yankee army, but to no material purpose. The foragers would first go to the houses and inquire of the families where they kept their provisions, horses, mules and such, the answer invariably being that "we'ens have none, are poor people," etc. The boys could not be fooled out of a good thing by such talk as that, but proceeded immediately to an investigation of the matter.

Drawing the rammers from their guns they would insert them in the ground at every suspicious place where fresh dirt might be seen, and if they should strike anything hard with them, the process of digging would be the next thing on the programme, and behold! various things of consecutive kinds would appear, probably the whole contents of a smoke-house or dwelling. The soldier, making this discovery, would take of the treasure what he wanted, and tell the next fellow he met, who, after satisfying his desires would do unto another as he was done by, fulfilling the moral rules. In this manner, the whole treasure would soon be absorbed in an arithmetical decreasing progression.

While some soldiers were pursuing this plan for finding things, others were pursuing other plans. Calling a negro, they would inquire where his *massa* or missus had hid their mules, the reply being, "I don't know, *massa*." "But you do know, you black rascal, now out with it, or you'll hear a dead nigger fall," at the same time presenting a gun. It works like a charm, the negro begs and agrees to tell. A Yankee can't be foiled, for he has more ways than a centipede has legs.

No sooner had our army reached the Savannah river than many of the foragers crossed it into South Carolina, on large flat-boats which they captured going down the river towards Savannah laden with the choicest treasures. There was also a small stern-wheel gun-boat plying along the river above Savannah, watching the movements of our forces, which General Morgan allowed his foragers would *gobble* before his command reached Savannah.

In going down the Savannah River, the division passed near old Ebenezer Church which was built in 1739, nearly one hundred and twenty-seven years ago. It is the remains of the oldest church in the United States, and bears with it much of historical interest.

On the afternoon of the 9th of December, when our column was within fourteen miles of Savannah, our passage was disputed by a rebel battery planted at the crossing of two roads.

Two regiments of our brigade, the Eighty-sixth and 125th Illinois, were deployed as skirmishers, with orders to advance until they found the enemy's works. By the time these orders were executed, night drew on, and under its cover the rebels retreated. This battery was captured, however, having mistaken the roads and running into other of our forces.

The Eighty-sixth regiment, in this skirmish, lost two men wounded. One from Company A, the other from H.

After the skirmish, our division marched to the Ten-mile House and went into camp, giving the road to the 20th Corps.

The next day, the command moved on to within three or four miles of Savannah, taking up position around it. The siege of this place may be said to have begun on the 11th of December.

The forces under rebel General Hardee in the works around Savannah numbered about fifteen thousand men.

The face of the country in this vicinity, was level and swampy, so that a large force well handled would make a formidable resistance.

Our works were built close up to the enemy's, and constant skirmishing went on.

On the 13th, two days after the siege began, the 2nd Division of the 15th Corps, charged on Fort McAllister and took it. This gained us communication with our fleet, and a short time after we eat hard tack from the great sea.

During the siege, the Eighty-sixth did not go on the front lines, but remained in camp in the rear, spending most of its time pounding rice or seeing it well done by the natives.

In the siege of Savannah, the 20th Corps held the left of our lines, resting on the Savannah River; the 14th Corps was on its right; the 17th Corps next, and the 15th Corps on the extreme right, with its flank resting on the Gulf railway, at station No. 1. The army remained in this position until the 21st, ten days from the commencement of the siege. In the meantime there was a deal of foraging done, as the country began to fail to supply the demands made upon it.

The last few days of the siege, the foragers were compelled to go a long distance to the rear in order to procure the necessary quota of rice, for this was eminently a rice country. The soldiers always had regular meals of rice and pork for breakfast, pork and rice for dinner, and *vice versa* for supper.

Up the Savannah River from the city of Savannah, and bordering on it upon either bank, were large and nourishing rice plantations, cultivated by great numbers of negroes of every hue of the skin and brogue of the tongue, some of them direct from Liberia, some from New Guinea, and others from the swamps of Florida. It was amusing to see the soldiers act the place of master and overseer over these deplorable creatures.

One soldier would crowd together thirty or forty of them, and march around them at right-shoulder-shift arms, keeping them at work pounding rice with mortar and pestle. Great ricks of this precious produce, in every way resembling oats, were stacked on each plantation, and from ten to twenty thousand bushels in a single stack-yard. Our army made use of it in various ways, much of it being threshed and hulled, and then used by the soldiers, but a greater part fed to mules.

Thus, things passed merrily on, until the memorable 21st of December, when our forces marched proudly into the "Forest City," Hardee having evacuated it on the night of the 20th. Now, the whole army went into camp in and about it, being once more in communication with the outer world.

Here ends the great raid to the sea.

Immediately after the capture of Savannah, General Sherman sent the following brief note to President Lincoln:

> I beg to present you, as a Christmas gift, the city of Savannah, with one hundred and fifty heavy guns and plenty of ammunition, and also about twenty-five thousand bales of cotton.

On this raid, the army marched over three hundred miles directly through the heart of Georgia, living off the best of the land. No less than ten thousand negroes left the plantations of their former masters and accompanied the army when it reached Savannah, without taking note of thousands more who were left along the line of march. Over twenty thousand bales of cotton were burned, besides twenty-five thousand captured at Savannah. Thirteen thousand head of beef cattle, nine million five hundred thousand pounds of corn, and ten million five hundred thousand of fodder, were taken from the country and issued to the men and animals.

Besides the history of this great raid, there are many other historical incidents connected with this portion of the country. Savannah itself was the first settlement in the State, being laid off in the year 1733. It was here where the great John Wesley first officiated as minister. And it was the scene of many revolutionary incidents; where General Lincoln fought the British in October, 1779; where Pulaski fell, and where Nathaniel Greene lies buried.

Savannah is located in a low, level country, surrounded by almost impassable swamps of a very unhealthy nature. It has a canal running into it from the Ogechee, and three railroads radiating from it; and from its beautiful shade trees, it is appropriately called the "Forest City."

Our great raid through Georgia, the Queen State of the Confederacy, was practically unobstructed by the enemy. True, they attempted to arrest our progress, but without the slightest success. Some of Wheeler's men, would, at times, make a stand behind an intrenchment and contest our advance. Our skirmishers would push forward, reinforced by the reserve, a charge would be sounded by the bugle, a rush follow—and amid the rattle of musketry and report of field pieces, the ground would be swept over by our boys, the works carried, and enemy routed. These little fights resulted in no check to our advancing columns. The head of the column would halt to let the rear close up, and before that was done, the advance guard would have cleared the way, and the column again set in motion.

Such too, was the case when fallen trees or destroyed bridges ob-

structed the road. The pioneers had usually cleared away the impedi-
ments before the column had closed up, and no stoppage on this account was experienced. Notwithstanding this arduous march down to
the great sea, the soldiers were not in the least dispirited. They wanted
for nothing to eat or wear, and it seemed to them more of a gala day
than one of fatigue.

Before closing this chapter, we will give a summary of events from
the time we left Lee and Gordon's Mills until the close of the year
1864.

The total casualties of the Eighty-sixth Illinois, during this time,
the most eventful period of its history, were:

Recruits	16
Transferred by promotion	1
Transferred to other regiments	26
Discharged 9 Ordinary deaths	7
Killed in action	45
Missing	25
Deserted	6
Wounded in action	113
Wounded accidental	8
Died of wounds	10
Surrendered from desertion	1
	————
Aggregate	267

The beginning of 1864 found us near Chattanooga with an army
nearly equal to our own to contend with; the end of it found us in Savannah, snugly encamped near the great sea. The whole year had been
resplendent with victory. Atlanta and Milledgeville and Savannah had
fallen, and the anaconda of Yankee vengeance had almost extinguished
the lights of rebellion. Success seemed mixed with doubt when the
year began; when it closed, bright and buoyant was the hope of our
armies on land and sea.

Sherman had pushed from the mountain districts of the north to
the level lowlands of the south; no army having ever met with more
signal success than his. No difficulties had been more successfully overcome, at any time or age, than by his exultant army. With determined
zeal and firm tread it marched from one victory to another.

If it failed in driving the enemy at one or two or three trials, it
was still fearless and determined. And he was a brave and mighty man

who led this army through so many perils to lasting fame and achievements. It had been on an active campaign for eight long months, digging in the dirt and marching like the wind.

CHAPTER 8

Battles of Averysboro and Bentonville

At Savannah, General Sherman received instructions from the Lieutenant General to embark his army on transports, and hasten to the James river, to participate in the final destruction of the main army of the rebellion. However, upon Sherman's earnest representation of the difficulty of moving sixty thousand infantry, and ten thousand cavalry, with their due allowance of artillery, so great a distance by water, and on assurance that he could place his army at the desired place sooner, in better condition, and with more injury to the enemy, General Grant consented to this modification, and gave the necessary orders.

A division was drawn from General Sheridan's army of the Shenandoah, and sent to Savannah as a garrison. This enabled Sherman to take with him the entire army with which he made the raid through Georgia. He determined to make the distance between Savannah and Goldsboro at one stride. Some time was consumed in preparation, and by the 15th of January, 1865, all was ready and the movement began.

On the 20th of this month, the 2nd Division of the 14th Corps, still under the command of James D. Morgan, moved out from Savannah eight miles in a north-western direction, camping near Tuly's Station, where the command lay wind-bound for four days.

Just a short time prior to this move from Savannah, General Feering was placed in command of the 3rd brigade, under General Morgan, thus relieving Colonel Langley of that command.

General Feering remained with his brigade, much beloved by all, until the battle of Bentonville, N.C., where he was wounded, being so disabled that he never afterwards resumed command of it. On the morning of the 25th, at seven a.m., the command resumed its march from Tuly's Station, the 14th Corps with Geary's division of the 20th, and Corse's division of the 15th Corps, marched up the west bank of the Savannah to Sister's ferry, where they crossed over to the South Carolina side, on the 5th of February, having been detained one week on account of high water at this ferry.

On the 8th, the division again cut loose from communications, marching up the Savannah to a point opposite Barnwell, where it left the river road and going to Barnwell, crossed the Salkahatchie river on its route. From Barnwell it took a northern course, striking the Augusta and Charleston railway at a small place known as Williston, thence, continuing north, crossed the South and North Edisto rivers, and going within one and a half miles of Columbia, was headed off by other troops, being compelled to move back up the Saluda River, some eight miles from Columbia, where, on the 26th, it crossed it on a pontoon bridge, and thence marching north-east, round Columbia, crossed Broad River at Fursell's Ferry, some twenty miles nearly north of Columbia. Our division was ferried over this stream, as there were not enough pontoon boats to complete a bridge. Crossing the river in the afternoon of the 18th, it went into camp, building breastworks for a protection to our supply train, as it was reported that Hood was also crossing the river above us.

Before going into camp, the eighty-sixth sent out a detail of foragers, under charge of Captain Hall, of Company H, to scour the rich country beyond the Broad river, meeting with more than ordinary success. This party had a skirmish with a squad of the enemy's *videttes*, driving them pell-mell.

As the army remained here a few days, we will review the most interesting events of the march up to this period.

The general features of the country over which the division passed, was that of a hilly, undulating plain, becoming more hilly and broken the farther north it went, until these undulations had gradually assumed the proportions of high hills. The country south of the North Edisto River, in Carolina, is far richer in its soil and yields a better crop than that north of this river.

The plantations, too, are larger, and lie more in a body than in other parts of the State over which we passed; and it is a curious fact, often remarked, that there is no rock or gravel here. The soil is seldom black, but usually a yellow clay of a spongy texture. North of the North Edisto River, the country begins to assume a stony and gravelly appearance, and rises in ridges of hills until it becomes very broken indeed.

There is a peculiarity in the soil of this part of the country which deserves remark. It is this: fields are sometimes seen covered over with a white sand, frequently an inch, and sometimes more, in depth. Off at a distance, a person unaccustomed to this peculiarity, would mistake this sand for a sheet of water. All soldiers are aware of this fact who have passed this portion of the country. There are places again where the sand seems to have been drifted like snow over the surface of a plain, and as much as one thing can resemble another, these drifts resemble snow, of a pure white colour.

The swamps in this State are very different from those of Georgia. They are not so difficult to travel through, and not near as numerous and large. In many of them, rice is extensively cultivated, and is far superior in quality to that raised on high lands.

So far, the State furnished us an abundance of forage of every kind, and the very best.

The boys lived sumptuously on flour, molasses, cured hams and many other of the staunch things of life—never fared better.

They always ate to satiety, and quit with plenty left. From the very first they treated South Carolina as her acts of treason and atrocity deserved. Nearly every house all over the country was fed on the flames of Yankee vengeance. When their houses were burnt, the proud chivalry were obliged to seek refuge in negro shanties—an awful condescension, but scores of them have had their pride thus broken.

To some, it may have seemed relentless barbarism to burn and devastate a country in the manner in which Carolina was served, but when they remember she was the main actor in the rebellion, fired the first gun, and led her sister States into a fratricidal war, and, moreover, prided herself in such acts of inhumanity, who then can pity her, or sympathize with her? She dared not ask sympathy, for multitudes of slain patriots answered, No sympathy for the venomous Carolina! There was no time in the day when looking around you there might not be seen liquid flames of fire lifting themselves in mad waves above the beautiful mansion, gin or fences; and even the hills and valleys for miles around were blue with smoke.

These were truly the smoky days of Carolina! Such was the inveterate hatred our troops entertained towards this State, and such the freedom allowed, that seldom the least of things were spared. If there was more forage than was needed for army consumption, the dancing

74

flames of Yankee vengeance eat it up.

This portion of South Carolina was not thickly settled, owing to single persons owning very large tracts of land. On nearly all of these extensive plantations there was usually two fine dwellings: one for the lord, the other for the overseer. Round the overseer's dwelling there was a large number of negro shanties, frequently from ten to fifty, somewhat resembling a town. The lord's residence was invariably fixed off in gay colours, with its handsome yards, out-buildings to break the summer's sun, with high walls inclosing a square for hounds, besides many other things. Then inside the dwelling itself were the costliest and most beautiful decorations imaginable. The richest Turkey carpet covered the floor; the finest sofas, chairs, tables, and other decorations filled the rooms, and a large and extensive library was invariably to be found. But these gay ornaments vanished before the "vandal Yanks," as the dewdrops before the rising sun.

The scenery from the high hills that border on the western bank of the Broad River, is grand in the extreme. Excepting that in the vicinity of Chattanooga, it surpasses anything of the kind that ever came under our observation. Looking eastward, you see the railroad and river winding their snake-like course along the high and hilly plain. And from the same view, as far as the eye can reach, one vast plain, undulating and broken, spreads itself before you, diversified with a green forest of pine, and fields covered with pure white sand, resembling high drifts of snow. Then around you, in whatever point of compass you should chance to look, thick volumes of smoke might be seen rising out of the valleys, over the tops of intervening hills, presenting a picturesque and novel scene.

Columbia, the capital of South Carolina, some twenty miles south of our position on Broad river, was captured on the 17th of February, by the right wing of the army, under General Howard, the mayor making a formal surrender of the place to Colonel Stone, commander of a brigade of the 15th Corps. This brigade was the first organized body to enter it. The city was fired by Wade Hampton's men before they left it, and nearly destroyed, notwithstanding the effort made by our troops to save it. While our division remained on the east side of the Broad river, it was engaged, for a time, in destroying the Spartansburg railway. It was a poor excuse for a road, the iron being old and worn out.

From Broad River, our column took up the line of march at six o'clock on the morning of February 20th, moving in a north-eastern direction, crossing Little river, and striking the Charlotte and Columbia railway at White Oak Station, four miles north of Winnsboro; thence marching up the railway some six miles, crossed it at Blackstakes, and marching east, camped at twelve m. on the 22nd, giving the road to the 20th Corps.

The march was resumed at eight a.m., on the 23rd, camping at night near Rocky Mount, on the Catawba river, in the north-eastern corner of Fairfield district. On the 24th, the Eighty-sixth Illinois was moved forward several miles, and camped on Rocky Mount, where it remained four days. The 14th Corps having crossed the Catawba river by the 28th, resumed the march. General Morgan's division now led the advance of the corps, and marching in a north-eastern course, crossed Flat, and the two Lyncher Creeks, and passing through Hickory Head on its route, arrived on the Great Pedee, at a point eight miles above Cheraw, where it laid a pontoon bridge, and crossed over on the 7th of March.

From the Great Pedee, the line of march was taken up in a direct course for Fayetteville, where the command arrived on the 11th of March.

The country between the Broad and Catawba rivers is very broken indeed. One ridge of hills closely succeeds another, and they are high and steep. The scenery here is exceedingly wild and romantic. There has been a romance written of this part of the State, of the era of the Revolution, called the Black Riders of the Congaree, which was interesting to read while we were also acting a great drama there. This was also the campaign grounds in the times of the Revolution. Rocky Mount, Camden, Sander's Creek and Hanging Rock are places of Revolutionary fame.

A great deal of trouble was experienced in completing a pontoon bridge across the Catawba, on account of heavy rains and high waters. By the time it would be nearly done the swift current would sweep it away. It was in consequence of this detention that General Sherman sent orders to General Davis, in case he could not get the pontoon bridge to hold by the morning of the 28th, to burn his trains, swim his mules, ferry his men and come on. But as good luck would have it, the bridge was finally made to stick, and on the 28th everything was landed safely on the other side.

About midnight on the 27th, Colonel Fahnestock blew his whistle for the regiment to fall in and cross the river. The winds blew and the rains fell, but for all that the Eighty-sixth had to crawl out of its dry tents, do them up and go; and when it reached the pontoon it was not yet done, causing us to lay round enjoying the benefit of the rain till morning. The Eighty-sixth about this time thought it would get a permanent detail as train guards, get to ride and such; but like many other of its hopes and plans, it was all "in a horn."

On the march from the Catawba there was a deal of corduroying to be done on the muddy roads, and by the time our long trains had passed over they were far worse than ever. Our corps train consisted of more than six hundred wagons, and when stretched out on the same road, as was very often the case, it would string out from six to seven miles, making bad roads for the rearmost wagons. General Davis was surprised at the rapidity with which General Morgan moved his command from the Catawba to the Great Pedee, and complimented him for it.

General Morgan was, in every sense of the word, a go-ahead man; he was so kind and careful with his men that they would speak of him altogether by the sobriquet of "Uncle Jimmy Morgan." He was odd and peculiar in his manner; he stood in a position inclining forward, and when he walked he held his hands behind him, his eyes striking the ground at an angle of forty-five degrees. In conversation with others, he walked rapidly backwards and forwards as if in great mental excitement, doubtless, as Artemus Ward would say, "a way he has." He was plain and unostentatious in his dress, wearing a soldier's blouse, a soldier's hat, and soldier's shoes, being a private soldier out and out, the only distinction consisting in the little star upon either shoulder—the insignia of his rank.

Those who did not know him would wonder what soldier that was using so much authority. General Morgan was not only common to and among his men, but, better than all, he was careful with them, and valued their lives as much as his own, never commanding them to go where he would not accompany them. Whenever there was a battle pending, you would see him on the skirmish line dodging round and looking about for himself; and when there was great danger, he would tell his boys to be very careful and not get hurt, seeming really to love them.

Before the general entered the service he was said to have been a pork packer, though there was another report that he was a Methodist preacher. These reports were often the source of amusing incidents. Frequently on our long marches the boys would become tired and worn out, wanting to go into camp. By and by Uncle Jimmy would come along while they were in this mood, when some mischievous fellow would cry out—not to the general, but that he might hear it: "I'll be d——d if I sell Uncle Jimmy my hogs if he don't camp pretty soon." This strikes the nail on the head; the general laughs and goes ahead, jerking the reins as usual. Uncle Jimmy was certainly a man of the finest feelings and respect for others, and possessed a true, brave and loyal heart.

In his order to his command, announcing the capture of Richmond, he said: "Let every true and loyal heart rejoice."

There was a marked peculiarity in the country between the Catawba and Pedee, consisting in a great many rocks scattered here and there of an enormous size and peculiar shape. They were from eight to twelve feet in height, of an oval form, and covered with a thick green moss.

These curious rocks excited the wonder of all. On one we saw there was a spring, with its bright waters trickling over its sides so beautiful and wonderful, and known as Hanging Rock of historic fame.

The country between the Great Pedee and Cape Fear Rivers is one vast, extensive pine forest. In this section there are but few plantations, and they are small. The general features are level, and the undulations, if any, are slight. Out of these forests, the inhabitants manufacture turpentine, rosin and tar in great quantities. They hew the bark from two sides of the tree, and near its roots cut a niche to receive the juice that does not gum on its sides. On nearly every stream there is a factory for the making of turpentine, rosin and tar. On our passage through, these factories were full, and when burning, made a huge fire and smoke, far surpassing in grandeur anything of the kind we ever saw, or ever expect to see.

Among the curiosities of our march, the burning of these factories was the most curious. Just imagine one hundred barrels of rosin and as many of turpentine and tar to be thrown together and ignited. It is impossible for a person who has not witnessed such a scene, to form a proper idea of the real grandeur and sublimity of these dense volumes of black, agitated smoke, brightened betimes with lofty flames of liquid fire, that seem to lift themselves in the fury of their madness to the very skies.

When our column was within twenty-four miles of Fayetteville, General Kilpatrick, who was several miles to the left of our division, was surprised by the enemy and routed, though he afterwards rallied his men and regained his camp.

The army now entered Fayetteville without further opposition, remaining from the 11th of March until the 15th. During its stay several small steamers came up from Wilmington, bringing provisions and mail.

The left wing of the army remained at Fayetteville the short space of four days, when it led out on the main road to Raleigh, which follows the right bank of the Cape Fear River some sixteen miles or more, and branching at Averysboro.

The supply train of the 14th Corps was left behind in charge of the 3rd Division, to intercept us by a nearer route whenever provisions enough arrived at Fayetteville to load it.

On the morning of the 16th the left wing moved from its camp of the night previous and discovered the enemy with artillery, infantry and cavalry, in an entrenched position in front of the point where the road branches off towards Goldsboro through Bentonville. Hardee, in retreating from Fayetteville, had halted in the narrow swamp neck between Cape Fear and South rivers, in the hope of holding Sherman there, in order to save time for the concentration of Johnston's army at some point in his rear. Hardee's force was estimated at twenty thousand men.

It was necessary to dislodge him, that our army might have the use of the Goldsboro road, as also to keep up the feint on Raleigh as long as possible. Slocum therefore advanced on his position, only difficult by reason of the nature of the ground, which was so soft that horses and men would sink everywhere and could scarcely make their way at all. The 20th Corps led the advance of Slocum's column, the 14th Corps following with Kilpatrick's cavalry in the entire advance.

The 20th Corps, upon finding the enemy, drove him from his first line of works, and advancing, took position confronting his second line, which was more formidable than the first. Then the 14th Corps took position on the left of the 20th Corps, our division being on the extreme left of the line, with its left resting on the Cape Fear river. The whole line now advanced late in the afternoon, drove the enemy well within his works, and pressed him so hard that he retreated during the night in a hard storm over the worst of roads. From this position Hardee retreated on Smithfield.

No member of the Eighty-sixth will forget with what difficulty it got its position in this battle, having to wade through creeks and swamps up to one's armpits. There was no chance to make a deflection to the right or left to shun a quagmire, right ahead being the only chance. The Eighty-sixth skirmishers in this engagement experienced a hard time; but the main body of the regiment was not brought into action.

The loss of the regiment was two killed and three wounded. The killed were Captain John F. French, of Co. K, and Rileigh George, of Co. F. Captain French was a brave and accomplished officer, and beloved by all the regiment. Co. K lost two wounded, and Co. C one. As soon as Hardee was known to have retreated, our forces were again put on the move, taking the road leading to the right, built a bridge across the swollen South River, and marched on the Goldsboro road.

Our wounded were taken with us from the battlefield of Averysboro, and as there were not enough ambulances for them, some were loaded in army wagons. The march was continued in the direction of Bentonville, over a country rich with forage of every kind except molasses—a luxury we were not often without. Meal and meat were to be had in abundance. No wanton destruction of property was tolerated in this section of the country, for there was too much loyalty and poverty for that, and soldiers are too magnanimous not to respect these; but where luxury and pomp abound, they are hyenas and wolves.

On the night of the 18th, our division camped on the Goldsboro road, about five miles from Bentonville and twenty-seven from Goldsboro, at a point where the road from Clinton to Smithfield crosses the Goldsboro road.

General Sherman had been with our wing of the army up to this time, and anticipating no more opposition in the occupation of Goldsboro, left General Slocum's column on the next morning to accompany Howard's advance into Goldsboro.

Early on the morning of the 19th, the 14th Corps, being in advance of the 20th on the same road, marched directly on to Bentonville. On arriving at that place it soon discovered the enemy in force, strongly intrenched on the further side of a difficult swamp.

The 1st Division, driving back his cavalry and skirmishers, took a position on the left of the road, and the 2nd division to the right of the same. These divisions set to work and built log breastworks.

As soon as General Slocum ascertained that the combined forces of Hoke, Hardee and Cheatham, all under command of rebel General Johnston, were massed in his front, he ordered the two divisions of the 20th Corps to form on the left of the 14th Corps, at the same time ordering up the two divisions that were back with the supply trains.

Meantime the enemy sallied out on the left flank of the 1st division of the 14th Corps, driving it back pell-mell, then pushing forward, struck the flank and rear of the 2nd Division.

At this juncture our brigade was moved out from the works on the double-quick to cover its left flank. Before it got its lines formed the rebels were upon it, and in the battle and confusion that ensued it was driven back, but forming again it threw up logs and rails for protection, which it held against six or seven successive charges.

The giving back of our brigade left exposed the rear of the other two brigades. These brigades were formed in two lines, and were now attacked furiously in front and rear. Therefore the rear line changed sides of its works, and thus the advance of the enemy was met from both ways. These brigades fought heroically, and after a most desperate engagement came out victors, severely chastising the enemy, and capturing over three hundred prisoners. It was about this stage of the game that the 20th Corps was brought up to our assistance, Johnston's forces driven back, and our lines mended. Our trains would certainly have been captured had it not been for the timely arrival of these fresh troops, for they were brought up close in the rear of the lines of battle, as there was no engagement with the enemy anticipated.

Finally, when the battle began to rage in all its fury, there arose a panic among them far surpassing what had happened in the fight. The approaching storm of the battle seemed to them to be against us, and the conclusion was, there was no safety but in flight. Teamsters began to flee to the rear with their teams, and ambulance drivers with their ambulances. Each tried to outrun the rest, for all were eager to be foremost; consequently, in the jumble and excitement that ensued, no headway could be made. In trying to head each other off, they stuck fast in the swamp. The drivers did not try to extricate their vehicles, but mounting mules fled for a serener sky.

There had certainly been a mixed time with the rear gentry as could be seen the next morning. From the time the enemy made his first attack until dark there was an incessant roar of artillery and musketry. It was the days of Chickamauga renewed. Our artillery did good execution, and its deafening roar was awful in that dismal swamp. Night ended this dreadful battle. It was fought in a low, difficult swamp, with mud and water over shoe mouth in depth, then it was densely covered with a thick growth of shrubs, briars and vines, closely interwoven. Judge the difficulty of such a place during a desperate engagement.

When the 3rd brigade was thrown out on the flank of the division, the Eighty-sixth Illinois was met by the enemy before it had formed its lines, Colonel Fahnestock ordering it to lie down and maintain its own, which it succeeded in doing for about ten minutes when the enemy struck it in flank, forcing it back several hundred yards, where it formed again and threw up a slight protection by means of logs and rails, with its left resting on the main road. Here it remained, holding its own, during the desperate charges made by Johnston on our lines.

In this day's fight, General Feering was wounded, and Colonel Langley took command of the brigade. Soon after the battle had ceased, the enemy fell back to his main line of works; our forces following up on the 20th, and taking position, built breastworks.

On the night of the 21st, General Johnston evacuated his intrenchments at this point, and retreated with his main force on Smithfield. Accordingly, on the morning of the 22nd, the 14th Corps having no enemy to oppose it, marched, and crossing the Neuse River on a pontoon, eight miles above Goldsboro, camped at that place, late at night of the same day. A few days previous to this, Generals Schofield and Terry had opened a line of communication to this place from Newbern.

The loss of the Eighty-sixth, in the battle of Bentonville, was, in all, two killed and twenty wounded.

The company loss was as follows:

Killed.

Company G	1
Company K	1
Total	2

Wounded.

Company B	1
Company C	1
Company E	2
Company G	6
Company H	4
Company I	1
Company K	5
Total	20

Here ends the second great raid.

The Eighty-sixth Illinois had traversed over five hundred miles, through all kinds of weather, country and scenery, and had consumed sixty-two days in doing it. Crossed no less than ten rivers, some of them at high water, and marched through the heart of South Carolina, leaving its mark behind it. Was engaged in several skirmishes and two battles, and lost twenty-seven men in battle and nine missing on the route, making thirty-six in all.

When it arrived in Goldsboro it was fat, ragged and saucy, having wanted for nothing but shoes. To get refitted, cleaned up and rested, were treats after the first order of things.

Before closing this chapter we will give an incident of the mode in which foraging was carried on during these great raids.

On every day's march, a detail was made from each company in our division to go in advance of the main column and forage for it. These men might be seen stringing out of camps long before the column was set in motion, and were, of course, the first to visit the plantations. The first things they would make a rush for, were the mules and horses, in order to carry a load away with them. Then, going to the houses, they would secure what provisions they wanted, and loading them into a cart, would set a negro to work hitching up a horse or mule to it, then putting him on the load to drive, leave a soldier with him to see things well done.

After this was done, some few of them would go back to the houses and rummage them from bottom to top, ransacking every nook and corner for all kinds of precious things. Trunks, boxes, beds and such, never escaped notice, their contents being thrown out on the floor and scattered to the four winds.

The same was the case with the fine libraries: books that were not wanted, were sent whirling on the floor. It was a caution to see them go in, paying no respect for anybody or anything. Beautiful damsels and affectionate dames stood around with eyes suffused with tears, pleading in vain. Negro houses met the same fate, for they too were turned topsy-turvy from one room to another. There was always some mean enough to do it, in the hope to find a fortune, and often his hopes were fulfilled, as the whites sometimes hid their money with the negroes, in the belief it would not be disturbed.

Out of one fine dwelling, on the Broad river, a soldier took eighteen thousand dollars in gold, and thinking that was all, set it on fire. After it had burned down and the fire died away, other curious soldiers took long poles and raking among the embers brought to light a large bucket of molten silver.

Though nearly every house on the line of march was rummaged for gold and silver, it was done by a few unprincipled men, who must needs accompany an army under all circumstances, ready for any dirty work to which their evil propensities may lead them.

After these foragers had collected what mules and horses they could find, and what provisions they wanted, they would travel on in the course the column was moving till near night, when they would halt until it came up, and all go into camp together.

CHAPTER 9

Capture of Johnston's Army

As soon as Sherman's army encamped at Goldsboro, it began to prepare for a new campaign. Nearly three weeks were required to refit and equip, and accumulate supplies necessary for the pursuit of Johnston's army, which was held well in hand about Smithfield.

On the 9th of April, an order was read to our division, from General Grant to General Sherman, directing him to move on Johnston and press him. Prior to this, an order had also been read, announcing the capture of Richmond, which created universal joy. Accordingly, early on the morning of the 10th of April, the army was set in motion against Johnston, whose entire force was estimated at thirty-five thousand effective men.

The 14th Corps marched up the eastern bank of the Neuse river, and arrived at Smithfield on the evening of the 11th. Johnston had rapidly retreated across the Neuse, and having his railway to lighten up his trains, could fall back faster than we could pursue. The rains had also set in, making the roads almost impassable, and rendering a deal of corduroying necessary.

On the morning of the 12th, the announcement of the surrender of rebel General R. E. Lee's entire army, was made to our corps, causing feelings of inexpressible joy. To us, it was great, grand and glorious news.

Upon this intelligence, General Sherman gave orders to drop all trains, and the army marched rapidly on to Raleigh where our division arrived in the afternoon of the 13th, Johnston's army having hastily retreated on the roads from Hillsboro to Greensboro. Remaining in Raleigh, over the night of the 13th, the 14th Corps, resumed the march on the 14th, moving south-west in the direction of Salisbury, Morgan's division arriving at Avon's Ferry on the Cape Fear river, on the afternoon of the 15th.

Thus matters stood when General Sherman received a communication from General Johnston that arrested all hostile movements for the time being. Our division now took up camp to await the results of negotiations between the commanders of the two opposing armies, which finally resulted in the surrender of Johnston's entire force.

The country between Goldsboro and Smithfield was usually low and swampy, affording good positions for the enemy's cavalry, which, in small force, and for a short time, would take advantage of them. On the contrary, however, the country between Smithfield and Raleigh was enchanting: we had not seen its equal in all the South. When our division was within fourteen miles of the city of Raleigh, a flag of truce train was sent to meet us, offering its surrender, which being accepted, the rest of the march was unobstructed according to conditions.

Kilpatrick's command was the first to enter it, and while the General was riding at the head of his men, some reprobate had the audacity to shoot at him. The offender was caught and hung.

The people of this place seemed glad that the "vandals" had come. Raleigh was the handsomest city in all famous Dixie, it being neat and clean, and its situation grand, the surrounding country affording an extensive view. Here was found many of the handsome feminine chivalry, who having fled before us from the line of our raids, finally concluded to meet face to face the "grim-visaged Yanks."

Our division now remained at Avon's Ferry, on the Cape Fear, five miles below the confluence of the Haw and Deep rivers, for five days, in a sickly swamp. At this place, the Eighty-sixth Illinois set to work and put up comfortable quarters, after which the boys lay round in the shade, discussing the prospects of a speedy peace, when by and by, someone brought the dreadful rumour of the assassination of President Lincoln, which became confirmed on the evening of the 18th, Sherman's order to that effect being read to our division.

This sad intelligence cast a deep gloom over their joy in the anticipations of peace. It was heard by every member of the regiment, and division, with feelings and expressions of the keenest sorrow.

Finally, a memorandum or basis of agreement, was drawn up by General Sherman, which, for the time being, was satisfactory to General Johnston and all present as a proposition to be submitted to the President of the United States for ratification or rejection, it being sent to Washington with all possible haste.

While these things were pending, our division was moved from the Cape Fear river to Holly Springs, on the 21st, that it might be nearer communications. When the memorandum between Sherman and Johnston was received by the cabinet at Washington, it was disapproved, and General Grant, with the following letter of instructions, was sent, in haste, to General Sherman:

War Department,
Washington City, April 21, 1865.

General: The memorandum or basis agreed upon between General Sherman and General Johnston having been submitted to the President, they are disapproved. You will give notice of the disapproval to General Sherman, and direct him to resume hostilities at the earliest moment.

The instructions given to you by the late President, Abraham Lincoln, on the 3rd of March, by my telegram of that date addressed to you, express substantially the views of President Andrew Johnson, and will be observed by General Sherman. A copy is herewith appended.

The President desires that you proceed immediately to the headquarters of General Sherman, and direct operations against the enemy.

Yours truly,

Edwin M. Stanton,
Secretary of War.

To Lieutenant-General Grant.

This dispatch was received on the morning of the 24th. General Sherman instantly gave notice to General Johnston as follows:

I have replies from Washington to my communication of the 18th. I am instructed to limit my operations to your immediate command, and not attempt civil negotiations. I therefore demand the surrender of your army on the same terms as were given to General Lee at Appomattox, Va., on the 9th of April, instant, purely and simply.

General Sherman now issued orders terminating the truce on the 26th, at 12 o'clock m., and ordered all to be in readiness to march at that time.

Again, on the 25th, General Johnston invited General Sherman to another conference, with a view to surrender. It now became the province of General Grant to take the lead in negotiations, but he preferred that Sherman should consummate the work. Nevertheless, General Johnston was afforded another interview. At this conference final terms were soon concluded, and the second grand army of the Confederacy was surrendered to Sherman on the following terms:

> All acts of war on the part of the troops under General Johnston's command to cease from this date. All arms and public property to be deposited at Greensboro, and delivered to an ordnance officer of the United States Army. Rolls of all officers and men to be made in duplicate, one copy to be retained by the commander of the troops, and the other to be given to an officer to be designated by General Sherman. Each officer and man to give his individual obligation in writing not to take up arms against the Government of the United States until properly released from this obligation. The side-arms of officers, and their private horses and baggage to be retained by them.
>
> This being done, all the officers and men will be permitted to return to their homes, not to be disturbed by the United States authorities so long as they observe their obligations and the law in force where they may reside.

Immediately on the conclusion of the definite cartel of surrender, General Sherman issued orders for the future movements of his army. Its work was done, and nothing remained for the greater portion of it not required to garrison the conquered country but to return home and disband.

The real and genuine feelings felt and expressed by the soldiers of our army at the surrender of Johnston, the return of peace, and the fact of their immediate march towards the homes from which they had been so long absent, cannot be written. It caused a thrill of emotions in every heart beyond the reach of the pen to portray.

The Eighty-sixth Illinois was still camped at Holly Springs when the glorious news of the fall of Johnston and the order for the homeward march was received. Every man was electrified with the great, grand and glorious news. Horrid visions of the past no longer possessed a single mind, but the hearty welcome, the joys and pleasures of a distant home, and the dear, beloved friends that made it home, crowded the mind of every one with inexpressible feelings of delight. Every man was more nimble, more talkative and more pleasant than ever before.

Nothing could be more enlivening, more vivifying and more devoutly to be wished than the very position in which they stood. Long and tedious marches had lost their dread, and every one became anxious to be homeward bound.

Bright visions of a future welcome at Peoria rose up before the minds of all—for there we would be met by the joys of our long absent friends, and the kind hospitality of the noble and generous-hearted ladies of the Women's National League—ladies who justly deserve our hearty thanks for their humane and loyal efforts to cheer and aid us in the field and at home. Their noble deeds will ever maintain a sacred spot on the tablets of our memory.

CHAPTER 10

Homeward Bound

General Morgan's division, of the 14th Corps, led out from its camp at Holly Springs at half past five o'clock on the morning of the 29th of April, and marching to the railroad camped near it, eight miles west of Raleigh, at Page's Station, where it procured supplies for its homeward march.

Remaining at this place until the 1st of May, it took up the march for the city of Richmond, and crossing the Neuse river at Fisher's Dam, camped on the first night four miles north of this dam and twenty miles from Oxford, after a hard march of twenty-two miles.

The column led out of camp the next morning at five o'clock a.m., and passing through Oxford, camped three miles north, marching twenty-three miles. Led out of camp on the morning of the 3rd, and being cut off by the 3rd Division of the 20th Corps, made a forced march round it, and came in ahead of its advance, but Morgan gave the road; then continuing on, camped on the Roanoke River, four miles into Virginia, having marched about eighteen miles.

Led out of camp on the 4th at half past three a.m., and crossing the Roanoke River at Faylor's Ferry, six miles above Huskington, on a pontoon bridge, marched through Boydton and camped on the Meherrin river. Marched twenty-three miles. Led out at five o'clock a.m. on the 5th; crossed Little and Big Meherrin Rivers, and marching through Lewiston, crossed Nottoway River and camped four miles from Nottoway C.H., having marched twenty-seven miles over bad roads. Resumed the march on the 6th at half past four o'clock, passing through Nottoway C.H. and Dennisville, camped late at night at Good's Bridge on the Appomattox River, having made a hard march of thirty miles under the pressure of a warm day.

Crossed the Appomattox River on the 7th, and marching camped on Falling Creek, five miles from Richmond. Made twenty-five miles. Now ended the march until the 11th.

It was a race between the corps commanders of Slocum's wing. Sherman ordered his Generals not to march over fifteen miles per day, but instead, General Davis made from twenty-two to thirty. It was an imposition of the worst feature, for many a good soldier was killed that might not have been, all for a foot race.

On this march the Eighty-sixth travelled one hundred and sixty-one miles over a beautiful country, in the latter part of spring, everything assuming a lovely aspect; and had the march been conducted as it was ordered to have been, it might have enjoyed the trip. All the inhabitants came out to see the Yankees; the old and young, the white and black, came from far and near to get a view. The regiment now set to work after its usual manner in the erection of comfortable quarters, which it had completed in a short time, and then took the world easy. It was encamped in a vicinity made renowned by the wars of the great rebellion, where the contending forces of the Rebel and Union armies had manoeuvred for so long a time for the mastery.

At this camp, it will be remembered, the commanding officers issued a deal of their surplus whisky to the division, which proved the harbinger of rows, riots, fights of a stirring and noisy kind, too numerous to mention. After four days rest, the division resumed its march for Washington City early on the morning of the 11th of May, and passing through Manchester, crossed the James river and entered the city of Richmond from the south-west. Now, for the first time, it beheld the once great Rebel Capital—the anaconda and boa-constrictor of rebel vengeance. When the command reached the north side of the James, the Libby prison could be seen on the right, where so many of our captured soldiers have languished and died under the cruel care of its keeper.

Then, a short distance above the Libby, and on the same side of the street, stood Castle Thunder, also a place of infamous reputation. Passing on, it was met by hundreds of peddlers dealing out their pies, cakes, cheese, and such, by the wholesale. The city did not show the ravages of war as much as was expected; true, a part of it had been burnt on its evacuation, but aside from this there was nothing to show that it had been so long the theatre of war; neither racked nor ruined, but compact, neat and clean.

All were surprised not to see huge entrenchments, high as the Chinese walls; but alas! there was nothing but an ordinary line of works around it, no stronger than the Eighty-sixth had often made on the Atlanta campaign in one night! "As strong as Richmond" had become a by-word. In front of Kenesaw, the Chattahoochie and Atlanta, may be found stronger works by far, thrown up in just one mortal night, than are to be seen on the south-west and north of Richmond.

Jeff. Davis, in his Sodom and Gomorrah of the Confederacy, was not as secure as many were wont to think. Sherman would have snaked him out sooner than he did if he had had his "flanking machine" in operating distance. But time progressed, the world moved, and Richmond fell.

Passing through Richmond, the command marching northward, camped four miles from Hanover C.H., making sixteen miles. Led out of camp at twelve o'clock M. on the 12th, and passing through Hanover C.H., crossed the Pamunky at Little Page's Bridge, and camped four miles above it, making eight miles. The course of march on the 13th was north-west, crossing the railway at Chesterfield, and camped one mile beyond Childsburg, making eighteen miles.

The march of the 14th was still north-west. The command camped on Plentiful creek by an old mill, having made an easy march of eighteen miles. Resuming the march on the 15th in a north-western direction, the command crossed the Rapidan River at Raccoon Ford, and camped for the night on the north bank, having marched seventeen miles. Led out of camp on the Rapidan at seven a.m. on the 16th, the Eighty-sixth Illinois being train guard and crossing the North Fork of the Rappahanock at Kellie's Ford, marched and camped near Catlet's Station, making twenty-two miles.

Marched from Catlett's Station at half past four a.m. on the 17th, and following the railway, passed through Manassas Junction and camped on the Bull Run battlefield, having marched twenty-five miles under a hot sun.

Resumed the march at five a.m. on the 18th, and passing through Fairfax C.H., camped within nine miles of Washington, having marched fifteen miles. Again, at nine a.m. on the 19th, the march was resumed, the command camping at a point equidistant from Washington and Alexandria, and four miles from each, having marched five miles. From its camp at this place the Eighty-sixth Illinois saw the distant dome of the Capitol for the first time.

Soon again the regiment had comfortable quarters, and enjoyed them hugely after so long and arduous a march. It marched one hundred and forty-four miles on its journey from Richmond to Washington, consuming eight days in doing it. On this march all were surprised not to find the country cut up with all kinds of works incident to war, for such things were not to be seen to any formidable extent. At Manassas Junction there were a few old forts, then in ruins, that may have been at some time quite formidable, but never wonderful. At Bull Run was to be seen the strongest entrenchments on the line of march, which had been built and held by the rebel army.

The following are the casualties of the regiment from the time it left Savannah until its muster out:

Recruits	6
Resigned	2
Transferred	5
Discharged	12
Ordinary deaths	4
Killed in action	3
Died of wounds	5
Missing in action	8
Wounded in action	20
Wounded, accidental	1
	——
Aggregate	66

Immediately upon the arrival of Sherman's army at Washington City, General Grant issued orders for the review of the Grand Army of the Potomac to take place on the 23rd, and that known as Sherman's army to take place on the 24th. Thousands of people flocked from all parts of the country to witness the grand pageant. The most ample preparations had been made for the occasion. The President was seated on an elevated stand, surrounded by his Cabinet officers, foreign ministers and distinguished strangers. Pennsylvania Avenue was lined on both sides from end to end with admiring people; every window presented its tableau of fair spectators; and the occasion was such as had never before been witnessed on the American continent. The daily papers all over the land soon flourished lively descriptions of the great and grand review; and according to them and the judgment of most of the spectators, the Army of the West bore off the palm; they described it as more graceful, more stalwart and more intelligent than the Grand Army of the Potomac.

On the occasion of this grand review of Sherman's army, a certain New York paper, the *Independent*, paid our division a very high compliment. It said:

> The finest looking set of men in either army—they were also
> said to be the best drilled—was the 2nd Division of the 14th
> Corps, composed of Western troops, and commanded by General James D. Morgan, of Quincy, Illinois, one of the bravest
> of the brave, the idol of his soldiers, and called by them 'Our
> Jimmy Morgan.'

But as for the soldiers themselves, grand pageantry in the line of
reviews had "played out." What was charming to the assembled multitude was no joyous affair to them. Their good time came, however,
when the attention of officials was turned to mustering out.

On the morning of the review of Sherman's army, our division led
out of its camp at an early hour, and by a slow and tiresome march it
arrived at Washington and passed before the admiring crowd between
one and three o'clock P.M., marching back to camp in the evening,
where it arrived as much fatigued as if it had been pursuing rebels.

At twelve o'clock m. on the day after the grand review, General
Morgan moved his division across the long bridge over the Potomac
into Washington City, and thence three miles north, where he camped
it near the President's summer houses.

While encamped here the boys were allowed many privileges in
and around the Capitol; all the guards being taken off, they were allowed to run wild, though they did not run riot.

Here also the Eighty-sixth Illinois, on the evening of the 6th of
June, 1865, was mustered out of the United States service, having been
engaged in the service of its country as an organized body for three
years wanting two months and twenty-two days.

Immediately after this the boys of the regiment saluted each other
as American citizens and not as soldiers, and though the metamorphosis was sudden, it seemed to have the force of a protracted transformation.

The following are the casualties of the regiment from the time it
left Lee and Gordon's Mills until its muster out:

Recruits	6
Transferred by promotion	1
Transferred to other regiments	31
Discharged	21
Ordinary deaths	11
Killed in action	48

Missing	33		
Deserted	6		
Wounded in action	133		
Wounded, accidental	9		
Died of wounds	15		
Resigned	2		
Surrendered from desertion	1		
	—		
Aggregate	323		

The entire casualties of the Eighty-sixth Regiment, during its term of service, in killed and died, discharged, transferred and deserted, was four hundred and sixty-seven men, the company loss being as follows:

	Killed and Died.	Discharged.	Transferred.	Deserted.
Company A	29	16	9	1
Company B	5	21	12	3
Company C	11	25	7	8
Company D	16	19	9	3
Company E	15	25	6	2
Company F	15	26	4	3
Company G	16	10	6	1
Company H	12	22	8	0
Company I	22	18	7	8
Company K	20	20	5	2
	—	—	—	—
Total	161	202	73	31

The regiment lost fifty-one men killed and one hundred and fifty-four wounded in battle, having participated in twenty-two engagements, not mentioning many others in which it rendered assistance by supporting, guarding flanks, or protecting rear. It marched thirty-five hundred and thirty miles, and was transported by railroad about two thousand miles, making a total distance of five thousand five hundred and thirty miles, besides a great deal of travelling about camps, on picket, etc., that is not taken into account.

There were three hundred and seventy-nine men mustered out with the regiment; besides this number there were many absent at hospitals and on detail who could not be present at the muster-out. Two days after it was mustered out of the service, the regiment boarded the cars, at the depot in Washington City, on its way to Chicago, there to receive its pay, disband and go home.

From Washington it passed through Baltimore *via* Harrisburg and Pittsburgh to Chicago, where it arrived at twelve o'clock m., on the 11th of June. Everywhere on its route it received expressions of the most cordial welcome. Everyone seemed rejoiced that the soldier boys were coming home from the bloody wars, in every way showing their grateful feeling of warmest sympathy for the services they had rendered to Union and liberty.

At Pittsburgh it received the kindest welcome of them all. More genuine sympathy was manifested there than the boys had yet experienced. In behalf of this people was engendered a feeling of the most profound regard. The regiment was escorted from the cars to the city hall by a band discoursing delightful music, where was prepared a dainty meal for all. After dinner, it was escorted back to the train, by the same band, amid the waving of handkerchiefs from the crowds that thronged the streets and balconies, and the "God bless you" from a thousand lips. So long as our minds can retrace the past, and so long as our hearts are capable of a generous emotion, will we continue to hold in sacred remembrance, the noble and generous-hearted people of Pittsburgh.

Every one anticipated a hearty welcome at Chicago, inasmuch as it had been extended elsewhere on the route; but we were cruelly and sadly disappointed. No one met the regiment at the depot even to tell it where to go. Every window presented its tableaux of fair spectators, but no signal was made in token of welcome, no hearty "God bless you" emanated in audible words from a single heart, but they gazed as if upon a menagerie of southern wild beasts. The men were chagrined, and would exclaim, "This is Richmond, not Chicago!"

The regiment finally found its way to Camp Fry and pitched its tents. Here it remained until the 21st, waiting impatiently for its pay and discharge.

The good folks of Chicago, however, determined not to allow the boys to leave their city until they had assuaged their anger. Accordingly, the Eighty-sixth and 125th Illinois received an invitation to appear at the Sanitary Fair rooms, and partake of the fatted calf, where they received not only a substantial dinner, but also several stirring speeches, among which was one made by General Sherman.

The general spoke as follows:

Fellow Soldiers: I regret that it has fallen to my task to speak to you, because, I would rather that others should do what is most common to them, and less so to me. But, my fellow soldiers, it gives me pleasure to assure you that what the President of this Fair has told you just now is true—that a hearty welcome awaits you wherever you go, not only in Chicago but everywhere. Many people think you want bread and meat, but your faces and my knowledge tell me that you prefer the waving of handkerchiefs and the applause of the people to all the bread and meat that fill the warehouses of Chicago. (*Cheers.*) Those soldiers who are now before me know where bread and meat can and will be found. (*Laughter.*) All we ask and all we have ever asked, is a silent and generous acknowledgment of our services when rendered in the cause of our country.

And, fellow soldiers, when you get home among those who will interest you more than anything I can say, just call to mind where you were twelve months ago. You remember the Kenesaw Peak and Little Kenesaw. It is not a year since you stormed them, and lost my old partner and friend, Dan. McCook. That was on the 27th June, 1864. In June, 1865, you stand in the midst of Chicago, surrounded by bright colours, and ladies, and children. Then you were lying in the mud, the rocks and the dirt, and you knew that there was an enemy we had to fight with and conquer, and we did not exactly know how to do it. (*Laughter.*)

But we were patient; we reconnoitered—we watched their flanks—we studied the ground—and in three days we had Johnston and his whole army pinned; he retired, and we did not give him a chance of stopping until he had put the Chattahoochie between us and him. That is a lesson to you. Temporary defeat is nothing when a man is determined to succeed. You are not conquered—you never can be conquered when the mind is clear and determined in its purpose; you must succeed—no temporary defeat can cause failure.

You will remember that on the 4th of July we stood close to each other, and we told them then that they would have to go farther than Atlanta, for we should continue to go on. (*Cheers.*) You will remember how their pickets told us they had reinforcements. Yes, but what? They had one of our Corps-Schofield's. (*Laughter.*) Before General Johnston knew, or dreamed of it, I had reinforced his side of the Chattahoochie by

General Schofield's 23rd Corps.

From this, my fellow soldiers I want you to learn the lesson, no matter where you are, today or tomorrow, by keeping a purpose close in your mind, in the end you will succeed, whether it be in military, civil, social or family affairs. Let no difficulty appal you—let no check alarm you—let your purpose in life be clear and steadfast—keep in view the object and design of your life, and just as sure as you are now before me in health and strength, you will succeed.

You are now returned to your homes, and the task now allotted to you is that of the future. The past is disposed of—it may soon be forgotten; but the future is before you, and that future will be more glorious than the past. Look at your own State of Illinois—look at the city of Chicago. It is hardly as old as any of you, for twenty-five years ago a little military garrison was here—a two-company post; and now it is a city of palaces, of streets, railroads, etc. You, the men of a city almost the second in the United States of America, are to assist in directing the affairs of this country.

You have the patience and industry, and more than that, you have organization, discipline and drill, and if I have been instrumental in teaching you this—in maintaining discipline, order and good government in the army which I have had the honour to command, I am contented; for on this system, and on the high tone of honour which pervades your minds, must be built the empire of America. (*Loud cheers.*)

I did not wish to address you, but I believe that there are no others here who desire to speak, and therefore I ask you to accept what is given in heartiness—a full, joyous, welcome home to Chicago. I know it is genuine, for I myself have experienced it. Feel you are at home—and that there are no more rebels, no more raking fire—no more shot; but that you have done with them all forever. Good morning.

On the afternoon of the 21st of June, having been in Chicago just ten days, every member of the Eighty-sixth received his pay and final discharge. Soon, the boys scattered to the four winds, bound for home and friends. Suddenly, the Eighty-sixth Illinois passed from existence!

Here ends the history of the good old Eighty-sixth Regiment of Volunteer Infantry, which had undergone so many days of hardships, perils and privations for the maintenance of home, union and liberty.

There is no surviving member of the regiment, but will always pride himself in having belonged to that organization; he will never forget the sad and repulsive scenes of the past, in connection with the merry days of yore; he will ever cherish in lasting remembrance the many noble and heroic comrades who have fallen by his side—men with whom he has passed the most trying hours of his existence—men who knowing the rights of their friends, their country and homes, dared raise the strong right arm in defence. Ay! he will ever invoke a just Heaven to reward them as their merit deserves, and in his hours of sad reflection, he will drop a tear to their memory.

REGIMENTAL ROSTER.

REGIMENTAL STAFF.

Colonel David D. Irons; August 27, 1862; died August 11, 1863, at Nashville, Tennessee.

Lieutenant-Colonel David W. Magee; August 27, 1862; resigned March 25, 1864, at Camp McAfee, Georgia.

Lieutenant-Colonel Allen F. Fahnestock; April 13, 1864; mustered out with regiment at Washington City.

Major J. S. Bean, August 27, 1862; resigned December 26, 1862, at Nashville, Tennessee.

Major O. Fountain; December 26, 1862; resigned October 30, 1863, at North Chickamauga.

Major J. F. Thomas; April 13, 1864; mustered out with regiment at Washington City.

Surgeon M. M. Hooton; August 27, 1862; mustered out with regiment at Washington City.

First Assistant Surgeon J. Gregory; August 27, 1862; transferred to U.S.C., December 15, 1863.

Second Assistant Surgeon I. J. Guth; August 21, 1862; mustered out with regiment at Washington City.

Adjutant J. E. Prescott; August 27, 1862; resigned December 26, 1862, at Nashville, Tennessee.

Adjutant C. D. Irons; ——; resigned April 25, 1863, at North Chickamauga.

Adjutant L. J. Dandy; ——; discharged April 25, 1865, per order War Department.

Regimental Quartermaster C. H. Dean; August 27, 1862; promoted A.Q.M., February 18, 1864.

Regimental Quartermaster A. Bracken; February 18, 1864; mustered out with regiment at Washington City.

Chaplain G. W. Brown; August 27, 1862; resigned October 13, 1863, at Nashville, Tennessee.

Chaplain J. S. Millsaps; October 13, 1863; mustered out with regiment at Washington City.

Non-Commissioned Staff.

Sergeant-Major L. J. Dandy; promoted.

Sergeant-Major D. E. Ward; mustered out with regiment.

Quartermaster Sergeant J. Adams; died February 19, 1863.

Quartermaster Sergeant C. Magee; mustered out with regiment.

Commissary Sergeant T. A. McNorris; discharged.

Commissary Sergeant W. J. Longfellow; mustered out with regiment.

Hospital Steward Jo. Robinson; mustered out with regiment.

Principal Musician A. Webber; mustered out with regiment.

Principal Musician S. B. Silzell; mustered out with regiment.

Company Officers

Company A.

Captain W. S. Magarity; August 27, 1862; resigned October 10, 1863.

First Lieutenant Jo. Major; August 27, 1862; promoted Captain October 10, 1863, and mustered out with regiment.

Second Lieutenant S. T. Rogers; Aug. 27, 1862; promoted First Lieutenant October 10, 1863, and resigned from wounds received in battle, June 27, 1864. J. J. Jones, promoted First Lieutenant.

Company B.

Captain E. C. Beasley; August 27, 1862; resigned January 28, 1863. J. P. Worrell, promoted Captain.

First Lieutenant J. C. Kingsley; August 27, 1862; mustered out with regiment at Washington City.

Second Lieutenant N. McVicker; August 27, 1862; resigned Jan. 17, 1863. P. W. Wycoff, promoted Second Lieutenant.

100

COMPANY C.

Captain J. F. Thomas; August 27, 1862; promoted Major, April 13, 1864, and mustered out with regiment. W. G. McDonald, promoted Captain.

First Lieutenant J. H. Batchelder; August 27, 1862; Brigade Commissary, and mustered out with regiment.

Second Lieutenant R. B. Beebe; August 27, 1862; resigned Feb. 1, 1863.

COMPANY D.

Captain Frank Hitchcock; August 27, 1862; mustered out with regiment at Washington City.

First Lieutenant W. D. Faulkner; August 27, 1862; mustered out with regiment at Washington City.

Second Lieutenant W. H. Hall; August 27, 1862; resigned Jan. 14, 1863. I. L. Gleares promoted Second Lieutenant.

COMPANY E.

Captain O. Fountain; August 27, 1862; promoted Major Dec. 26, 1862. J. F. Waldrof, Captain, resigned June 18, 1863. E. Van Antwerp, Captain, died July 15, 1864.

First Lieutenant M. Grave; August 27, 1862; resigned January 13, 1863.

Second Lieutenant S. W. Williams; August 27, 1862; resigned January 11, 1863. H. W. Wilson promoted First Lieutenant.

COMPANY F.

Captain J. L. Burkhalter; August 27, 1862; mustered out with regiment at Washington City.

First Lieutenant N. D. Combs; August 27, 1862; resigned January 11, 1863.

Second Lieutenant John Hall; August 27, 1862; promoted First Lieutenant, and mustered out with regiment at Washington City. A. P. Loveland promoted Second Lieutenant.

COMPANY G.

Captain W. B. Bogardus; August 27, 1862; died of wounds received in battle March 19, 1865.

First Lieutenant S. L. Zinser; August 27, 1862; promoted Captain; mustered out with regiment.

Second Lieutenant M. Kingman; August 27, 1862; promoted First Lieutenant; mustered out with regiment.

COMPANY H.

Captain J. H. Hall; August 27, 1862; mustered out with regiment at Washington City.

First Lieutenant E. E. Peters; August 27, 1862; resigned July 12, 1863. W. F. Hodge promoted First Lieutenant.

Second Lieutenant D. W. Merwin; August 27, 1862.

COMPANY I.

Captain A. L. Fahnestock; August 27, 1862; promoted Major January 31, 1864.

First Lieutenant A. A. Lee; August 27, 1862; promoted Captain Jan. 31, 1864.

Second Lieutenant J. L. Fahnestock; August 27, 1862; resigned Jan. 23, 1863. R. W. Groninger promoted Second Lieutenant.

COMPANY K.

Captain J. F. French; August 27, 1862; killed March 16, 1865. L. A. Ross promoted Captain.

First Lieutenant J. B. Pete; August 27, 1862; discharged Dec. 24, 1864.

Second Lieutenant H. F. Irwin; August 27, 1862; dishonourably discharged Nov. 29, 1862. John Morrow promoted Second Lieutenant.

Incidents and Anecdotes

CAPTAIN BURKHALTER'S ADVENTURE

On the morning of the 20th of August, 1864, while our army was besieging Atlanta, General James D. Morgan's division was ordered on a raid to cut the Montgomery and Atlanta Railroad. Our brigade, the 3rd, left its baggage in the rifle pits, leaving a sufficient guard with it. The skirmishers were also left on duty under the command of Capain Burkhalter, the subject of our narrative.

Sometime after the division had gone, the captain became lonesome and anxious to know what the division was doing, so he attempted to follow and see the fun. He followed it very well until within three or four miles of the railroad, when a heavy rain overtook him; he stopped under the shelter of a large tree until the storm had somewhat subsided, then mounting his horse pursued what he supposed to be the right road, but the pelting rain had obliterated every vestige of our course, and he in consequence was in a dilemma as to what was best. It did not seem well to turn back after having gone so far, so he determined to follow in the probable course of the column until he found more evidence one way or the other. On he went in a musing mood, doubting as he went.

Having now gone a long distance without any favourable signs, he had about concluded to return, when on a sudden a stalwart rebel, armed to the teeth, stepped out from behind a tree and commanded the unwary Captain to surrender. A complete surprise. What could he do; he had left his sword and pistol in camp, not dreaming of this adventure.

He stopped instanter, obeying the summons of his captor, for there was no other alternative; he was powerless. The next demand made of him was his watch and pocket book.

The rebel, for a short distance, marched the captain a few paces

103

in front, following close in the rear with a cocked gun, and leading the horse by the reins; but this was not getting along fast enough, for the horse would not lead good. He now ordered the captain on horseback, still walking close behind and directing the course of the prisoner by proper military commands.

They had thus travelled about two miles when a horseman was heard to approach on a keen trot from the direction of their front. This horseman was supposed to be a rebel cavalryman, but on coming closer he was discovered to be a Yankee. The rebel levelled his gun on him and commanded his surrender; but saying nothing, the Yankee threw the reins loose on the horse's neck and approached to the rebel's gun as if to give up, but seizing it thrust it to one side, when off it went, hurting no one.

The rebel was now at their mercy, if they could catch him, for he took leg-bail. Both the Yankees pursued and finally captured him. The orderly—for the last character was the captain's orderly—tried to shoot the fugitive, but his pistol would not go off.

Having captured the rebel, the captain loaded his gun and demanded back all that had been taken from him. The captain soon after found the column, bringing his captive with him, rejoicing—the rebel fighting mad.

Soldiers' Letters

Letters are the soldier's tonic. They will strengthen and restore when army grub and other restoratives, duly proportioned, wholly fail. The blues and all kinds of contagious diseases to which mortals are heir, caused by idleness and the lack of proper diversion of the mind, are soon uprooted by a good interesting letter from a fellow's most affectionate. Give soldiers full rations and regular mail, then there can nowhere be found a more rational set of men than they. But letters are sometimes like our crackers and pork, unfit for use.

Such letters do no good—they are no good. There is a sheet full of writing, to be sure, but it is about something that neither interests nor concerns us. Those letters that tell us about the little things of home; the farm, the horses, the cattle, the dogs and cats, their quality and disposition; also the parties and frolics, who is going to see who, and what people say about it, are the very letters that do all this good I have been telling about.

The soldiers will always crowd around the ones who get such letters, make remarks and ludicrous suggestions which cause bursts of hearty laughter and strains of highest merriment, thus passing the tedious hours of camp life in a light and merry way.

No one cares for a letter which is wholly devoted to the praise and admiration of one's patriotism and to the sacredness of the Union cause.

Such letters bore to the very quick. It seems to them that the writer is taking that opportunity to speak a word of eulogy for himself. As for the true soldier, he never asks for words of flattery; he is not to be gulled with bland words and braggadocio. The letter for the soldier is the long, pithy one, full of little things, even down to gossip. *Gossip is better than eulogy*, especially when used in an egotistical manner.

BATTLE

Much has been said and written about battle, the greater portion of which is an exaggeration of facts. Fireside writers and reporters have composed long manuscripts, beginning and ending in frantic agonies and seas of blood, exhausting the vocabulary of pathetic epithets. That battle is dreadful cannot be denied, but those who have passed through the fiery ordeal do not experience half the convulsions and agony of soul that is written. If a comrade falls, the column still moves on. No one, by the late rules of war, dare stop to bear off the wounded or sympathize with those in the throes of death. There are men detailed for that purpose, who follow up in the rear and give those in need due attention.

A soldier in a pitched battle does not pretend to know who is hurt until the battle is ended; he must needs push ahead and do his part until he is no longer able. Many of your comrades fall around you; they show unmistakable symptoms of severe wounds, but your attention is too much engrossed to ever think to inquire the nature of their wounds. You are hardly conscious of any suffering around you. Excitement has borne you off so that you never think to look and see who is on your right or left, or whose spirit is winging its flight from the body over which you are walking.

The soldier does not seem to feel pangs of sorrow when arms clash the loudest; he does not see danger and suffering and ghastly sights until all is over and quiet restored. Those who are unacquainted with the mental condition of the soldier in time of battle, wonder and ask why it is that those whom he knows so intimately are wounded and many times killed by his side without knowing the nature of their wounds or the circumstances of their death. The reason for this is manifest from what has already been said.

There is oftentimes more horror in the idea and dread of battle than in the thing itself. The soldier becomes so accustomed to human butchery that it loses many, very many, of its horrors.

After battle, when the clash of arms has ceased, is when the soldier's sympathy is tried. The solicitations of the maimed and dying raise a feeling of commiseration in the most obdurate heart; and still this feeling is of but short duration and of a mild character.

FARMING IN THE SOUTH

Farming in the Southern States is carried on in a very simple and seeming ignorant style. One could not refrain from laughing at their oddity in agricultural pursuits. They are a great many years behind the North in this respect, as well as in many others.

The whites and negroes are so sluggish, indolent and careless in their habits that their works are a fair prototype of themselves. There is a difference between a farm and a plantation, though they are carried on in nearly the same style; the main difference is that the one is gotten up on a larger scale than the other. What is usually called a farm is owned by a poor white man—while the plantation is owned by a wealthy planter, with his hundreds of negroes. The farm is known by its small area, by its improvements and its little old log house with its appendages; the plantation, by its vast area, its stately mansion and numerous negro shanties.

The improvements are usually very poor, with but few conveniences. On every plantation you will see a cotton press and gin house, with the stable under the latter. The cotton press is the first thing you get your eyes on when you approach a plantation, and then the gin house next. And as for the farms or little plantations, you scarcely know anything about them until you have them suddenly spread before your view. There is hardly ever anything external to warn one of their presence.

It is, as it were, a swath mown in the deep pine forest—the labour of a poor ignorant being, who, like the parrot, can talk and palaver with simple unmeaningness, but ignorant of the world beyond a radius of ten miles. The people, for the most part, break up their ground with one horse or ox, as the case may be, their plows being suited to the purpose.

This small plough is made after the fashion of our large two-horse breaking ploughs, and is, as we are wont to say, right or left handed.

Some farmers are too poor to afford a horse or mule; in this case they work an ox as if he were a horse, hitch him to the plough and drive him with ropes attached to his horns with as much precision as a horse or mule.

The oxen here may be of a more docile breed than found in our parts, and certainly are, for it would be dangerous with us to hitch one to a plough and start him on a row through a cornfield, for he would likely jump the fence before he reached the other end.

The rows of corn here are usually six feet apart, with a row of negro beans between. If one man can tend eight acres he thinks he is doing good business; the corn is hardly ever ploughed, it being worked with the hoe for the most part.

The women work in the field as well as the men, they being used to it. They will not believe us when we tell them that our women do not work in the field. When an acre of ground yields twelve bushels of corn it is thought to be a fine crop. They gape with wonder when we tell them we break our ground with two horses, plough our corn with a plough on which we can ride; that one man can tend forty acres and raise forty bushels to the acre. When we tell them about our reapers, our vast fields of wheat, oats, etc., etc., they gape, and wonder what we do with it all. If we tell them about our large prairies, rich soil and productive land, they wonder why they had not heard of that before.

Their principal diet is corn bread, meat and negro beans. These nigger beans, by the way, are not so bad, just the thing for the soldier; many farmers raise them altogether, so to speak. It is a common thing to see cribs of these beans as you pass through the country; it takes them so short a time to cook, which adapts them to our use. Corn and beans are not their only productions, for they sometimes grow a little wheat, oats, tobacco and cotton. Many reap their grain with the sickle, not having known the existence of the cradle. There are no reapers to be seen, or if at all, but seldom.

As a people, they have no enterprise; they live only to eat, and even that is done in a poor, unhandy style.

There are a great many turpentine, rosin and tar factories in "the sunny land of Dixie." There are vast tracts of land here, covered with dense forests of pine, that can be put to no other use than the production of these things. In North Carolina these factories are most numerous. They are built on small streams of water, and for miles around the trees are hewn on two sides; the turpentine running out, gums on the tree where it is hewn. On our march we burned many of these factories; they made a grand, huge smoke, most sublime.

It is impossible for a person who has not seen the like to form a proper idea of the real grandeur and sublimity of these dense volumes of black, agitated smoke, brightened betimes with lofty flames of liquid fire that seem to lift themselves in the fury of their madness to the very skies.

Rebel Letter

This letter, written by a rebel soldier, was found on the battle-ground at Bentonville, N. C.

Bivouac Near "Raccoon Ford," Va.,
September 25th, 1863.

Dear Coon—I have just received your kind favour of the 8th inst., and am very much gratified with its contents. I could not expect a long letter from a soldier "in the field," and I suppose your time was fully taken up reorganizing your company and regiment.

Since last writing you we had some little excitement ourselves. The Yankee, Meade, has tried to take advantage of our supposed decimated army, and has advanced across the Rappahannock River to the banks of the Rapidan. We have here checked his advance and are awaiting the attack which he is very slow about making. I think both sides are awaiting the decision of the battle in Tennessee and Georgia before a move is made.

We are daily in receipt of glorious news from Bragg, but there are so many rumours without foundation that we hardly know what he has done. I hope he will not rest until he has driven the foe across the Ohio. You have our brag fighting general with you now, and I know you will be victorious.

I have not heard a word from "Miss Mattie" since I left home, and if the truth must be told, I never want to again. I have found a new sweetheart, and I think the change is more agreeable, at least to me. I suppose you know that Miss Katie Furlow's father is running for Governor; of course you will support him.

You recollect that pretty little woman that I showed you in the theatre in Augusta, the one I said was the *belle* of Augusta-Miss Fannie Hatch. Well, I have been told by one who knows and believes, that "Albert," who performed with the "Queen Sisters" that night, has betrayed her. I can scarcely believe that so much loveliness would have fallen so easily, yet they say 'tis true.

I shall anxiously wait to hear further from you in reference to the lieutenancy. If you are successful in securing it for me (which I hope and pray you may be,) I shall be ever grateful to you.

I have not seen Joe Holt since the reception of yours, his regiment being on picket guard. I know he would send you his kind regards, if he knew I was writing to you. Accept my best wishes, and believe me to be

Truly your Friend,

A. Kent Bisel.

P.S.—Please direct to Co. "K," 4th Georgia, Dole's Brigade, Rhodes' Division, Ewell's Corps, A.N.V., and always to Richmond, Virginia.

LEONAUR

ALSO FROM LEONAUR
AVAILABLE IN SOFTCOVER OR HARDCOVER WITH DUST JACKET

THE FALL OF THE MOGHUL EMPIRE OF HINDUSTAN *by H. G. Keene*—By the beginning of the nineteenth century, as British and Indian armies under Lake and Wellesley dominated the scene, a little over half a century of conflict brought the Moghul Empire to its knees.

LADY SALE'S AFGHANISTAN *by Florentia Sale*—An Indomitable Victorian Lady's Account of the Retreat from Kabul During the First Afghan War.

THE CAMPAIGN OF MAGENTA AND SOLFERINO 1859 *by Harold Carmichael Wylly*—The Decisive Conflict for the Unification of Italy.

FRENCH'S CAVALRY CAMPAIGN *by J. G. Maydon*—A Special Correspondent's View of British Army Mounted Troops During the Boer War.

CAVALRY AT WATERLOO *by Sir Evelyn Wood*—British Mounted Troops During the Campaign of 1815.

THE SUBALTERN *by George Robert Gleig*—The Experiences of an Officer of the 85th Light Infantry During the Peninsular War.

NAPOLEON AT BAY, 1814 *by F. Loraine Petre*—The Campaigns to the Fall of the First Empire.

NAPOLEON AND THE CAMPAIGN OF 1806 *by Colonel Vachée*—The Napoleonic Method of Organisation and Command to the Battles of Jena & Auerstädt.

THE COMPLETE ADVENTURES IN THE CONNAUGHT RANGERS *by William Grattan*—The 88th Regiment during the Napoleonic Wars by a Serving Officer.

BUGLER AND OFFICER OF THE RIFLES *by William Green & Harry Smith*—With the 95th (Rifles) during the Peninsular & Waterloo Campaigns of the Napoleonic Wars.

NAPOLEONIC WAR STORIES *by Sir Arthur Quiller-Couch*—Tales of soldiers, spies, battles & sieges from the Peninsular & Waterloo campaigns.

CAPTAIN OF THE 95TH (RIFLES) *by Jonathan Leach*—An officer of Wellington's sharpshooters during the Peninsular, South of France and Waterloo campaigns of the Napoleonic wars.

RIFLEMAN COSTELLO *by Edward Costello*—The adventures of a soldier of the 95th (Rifles) in the Peninsular & Waterloo Campaigns of the Napoleonic wars.

LEONAUR

ALSO FROM LEONAUR

AVAILABLE IN SOFTCOVER OR HARDCOVER WITH DUST JACKET

AT THEM WITH THE BAYONET *by Donald F. Featherstone*—The first Anglo-Sikh War 1845-1846.

STEPHEN CRANE'S BATTLES *by Stephen Crane*—Nine Decisive Battles Recounted by the Author of 'The Red Badge of Courage'.

THE GURKHA WAR *by H. T. Prinsep*—The Anglo-Nepalese Conflict in North East India 1814-1816.

FIRE & BLOOD *by G. R. Gleig*—The burning of Washington & the battle of New Orleans, 1814, through the eyes of a young British soldier.

SOUND ADVANCE! *by Joseph Anderson*—Experiences of an officer of HM 50th regiment in Australia, Burma & the Gwalior war.

THE CAMPAIGN OF THE INDUS *by Thomas Holdsworth*—Experiences of a British Officer of the 2nd (Queen's Royal) Regiment in the Campaign to Place Shah Shuja on the Throne of Afghanistan 1838 - 1840.

WITH THE MADRAS EUROPEAN REGIMENT IN BURMA *by John Butler*—The Experiences of an Officer of the Honourable East India Company's Army During the First Anglo-Burmese War 1824 - 1826.

IN ZULULAND WITH THE BRITISH ARMY *by Charles L. Norris-Newman*—The Anglo-Zulu war of 1879 through the first-hand experiences of a special correspondent.

BESIEGED IN LUCKNOW *by Martin Richard Gubbins*—The first Anglo-Sikh War 1845-1846.

A TIGER ON HORSEBACK *by L. March Phillips*—The Experiences of a Trooper & Officer of Rimington's Guides - The Tigers - during the Anglo-Boer war 1899 - 1902.

SEPOYS, SIEGE & STORM *by Charles John Griffiths*—The Experiences of a young officer of H.M.'s 61st Regiment at Ferozepore, Delhi ridge and at the fall of Delhi during the Indian mutiny 1857.

CAMPAIGNING IN ZULULAND *by W. E. Montague*—Experiences on campaign during the Zulu war of 1879 with the 94th Regiment.

THE STORY OF THE GUIDES *by G.J. Younghusband*—The Exploits of the Soldiers of the famous Indian Army Regiment from the northwest frontier 1847 - 1900.

LEONAUR

ALSO FROM LEONAUR
AVAILABLE IN SOFTCOVER OR HARDCOVER WITH DUST JACKET

ADVENTURES OF A YOUNG RIFLEMAN by Johann Christian Maempel—The Experiences of a Saxon in the French & British Armies During the Napoleonic Wars.

THE HUSSAR by Norbert Landsheit & G. R. Gleig—A German Cavalryman in British Service Throughout the Napoleonic Wars.

RECOLLECTIONS OF THE PENINSULA by Moyle Sherer—An Officer of the 34th Regiment of Foot—'The Cumberland Gentlemen'—on Campaign Against Napoleon's French Army in Spain.

MARINE OF REVOLUTION & CONSULATE by Moreau de Jonnès—The Recollections of a French Soldier of the Revolutionary Wars 1791-1804.

GENTLEMEN IN RED by John Dobbs & Robert Knowles—Two Accounts of British Infantry Officers During the Peninsular War Recollections of an Old 52nd Man by John Dobbs An Officer of Fusiliers by Robert Knowles.

CORPORAL BROWN'S CAMPAIGNS IN THE LOW COUNTRIES by Robert Brown—Recollections of a Coldstream Guard in the Early Campaigns Against Revolutionary France 1793-1795.

THE 7TH (QUEENS OWN) HUSSARS: Volume 2—1793-1815 by C. R. B. Barrett—During the Campaigns in the Low Countries & the Peninsula and Waterloo Campaigns of the Napoleonic Wars. Volume 2: 1793-1815.

THE MARENGO CAMPAIGN 1800 by Herbert H. Sargent—The Victory that Completed the Austrian Defeat in Italy.

DONALDSON OF THE 94TH—SCOTS BRIGADE by Joseph Donaldson—The Recollections of a Soldier During the Peninsula & South of France Campaigns of the Napoleonic Wars.

A CONSCRIPT FOR EMPIRE by Philippe as told to Johann Christian Maempel—The Experiences of a Young German Conscript During the Napoleonic Wars.

JOURNAL OF THE CAMPAIGN OF 1815 by Alexander Cavalié Mercer—The Experiences of an Officer of the Royal Horse Artillery During the Waterloo Campaign.

NAPOLEON'S CAMPAIGNS IN POLAND 1806-7 by Robert Wilson—The campaign in Poland from the Russian side of the conflict.

LEONAUR

ALSO FROM LEONAUR
AVAILABLE IN SOFTCOVER OR HARDCOVER WITH DUST JACKET

BUGEAUD: A PACK WITH A BATON by *Thomas Robert Bugeaud*—The Early Campaigns of a Soldier of Napoleon's Army Who Would Become a Marshal of France.

WATERLOO RECOLLECTIONS by *Frederick Llewellyn*—Rare First Hand Accounts, Letters, Reports and Retellings from the Campaign of 1815.

SERGEANT NICOL by *Daniel Nicol*—The Experiences of a Gordon Highlander During the Napoleonic Wars in Egypt, the Peninsula and France.

THE JENA CAMPAIGN: 1806 by *F. N. Maude*—The Twin Battles of Jena & Auerstadt Between Napoleon's French and the Prussian Army.

PRIVATE O'NEIL by *Charles O'Neil*—The recollections of an Irish Rogue of H. M. 28th Regt.—The Slashers—during the Peninsula & Waterloo campaigns of the Napoleonic war.

ROYAL HIGHLANDER by *James Anton*—A soldier of H.M 42nd (Royal) Highlanders during the Peninsular, South of France & Waterloo Campaigns of the Napoleonic Wars.

CAPTAIN BLAZE by *Elzéar Blaze*—Life in Napoleons Army.

LEJEUNE VOLUME 1 by *Louis-François Lejeune*—The Napoleonic Wars through the Experiences of an Officer on Berthier's Staff.

LEJEUNE VOLUME 2 by *Louis-François Lejeune*—The Napoleonic Wars through the Experiences of an Officer on Berthier's Staff.

CAPTAIN COIGNET by *Jean-Roch Coignet*—A Soldier of Napoleon's Imperial Guard from the Italian Campaign to Russia and Waterloo.

FUSILIER COOPER by *John S. Cooper*—Experiences in the 7th (Royal) Fusiliers During the Peninsular Campaign of the Napoleonic Wars and the American Campaign to New Orleans.

FIGHTING NAPOLEON'S EMPIRE by *Joseph Anderson*—The Campaigns of a British Infantryman in Italy, Egypt, the Peninsular & the West Indies During the Napoleonic Wars.

CHASSEUR BARRES by *Jean-Baptiste Barres*—The experiences of a French Infantryman of the Imperial Guard at Austerlitz, Jena, Eylau, Friedland, in the Peninsular, Lutzen, Bautzen, Zinnwald and Hanau during the Napoleonic Wars.

LEONAUR

ALSO FROM LEONAUR
AVAILABLE IN SOFTCOVER OR HARDCOVER WITH DUST JACKET

CAPTAIN COIGNET *by Jean-Roch Coignet*—A Soldier of Napoleon's Imperial Guard from the Italian Campaign to Russia and Waterloo.

HUSSAR ROCCA *by Albert Jean Michel de Rocca*—A French cavalry officer's experiences of the Napoleonic Wars and his views on the Peninsular Campaigns against the Spanish, British And Guerilla Armies.

MARINES TO 95TH (RIFLES) *by Thomas Fernyhough*—The military experiences of Robert Fernyhough during the Napoleonic Wars.

LIGHT BOB *by Robert Blakeney*—The experiences of a young officer in H.M 28th & 36th regiments of the British Infantry during the Peninsular Campaign of the Napoleonic Wars 1804 - 1814.

WITH WELLINGTON'S LIGHT CAVALRY *by William Tomkinson*—The Experiences of an officer of the 16th Light Dragoons in the Peninsular and Waterloo campaigns of the Napoleonic Wars.

SERGEANT BOURGOGNE *by Adrien Bourgogne*—With Napoleon's Imperial Guard in the Russian Campaign and on the Retreat from Moscow 1812 - 13.

SURTEES OF THE 95TH (RIFLES) *by William Surtees*—A Soldier of the 95th (Rifles) in the Peninsular campaign of the Napoleonic Wars.

SWORDS OF HONOUR *by Henry Newbolt & Stanley L. Wood*—The Careers of Six Outstanding Officers from the Napoleonic Wars, the Wars for India and the American Civil War.

ENSIGN BELL IN THE PENINSULAR WAR *by George Bell*—The Experiences of a young British Soldier of the 34th Regiment 'The Cumberland Gentlemen' in the Napoleonic wars.

HUSSAR IN WINTER *by Alexander Gordon*—A British Cavalry Officer during the retreat to Corunna in the Peninsular campaign of the Napoleonic Wars.

THE COMPLEAT RIFLEMAN HARRIS *by Benjamin Harris as told to and transcribed by Captain Henry Curling, 52nd Regt. of Foot*—The adventures of a soldier of the 95th (Rifles) during the Peninsular Campaign of the Napoleonic Wars.

THE ADVENTURES OF A LIGHT DRAGOON *by George Farmer & G.R. Gleig*—A cavalryman during the Peninsular & Waterloo Campaigns, in captivity & at the siege of Bhurtpore, India.

LEONAUR

ALSO FROM LEONAUR
AVAILABLE IN SOFTCOVER OR HARDCOVER WITH DUST JACKET

THE LIFE OF THE REAL BRIGADIER GERARD VOLUME 1—THE YOUNG HUSSAR 1782-1807 *by Jean-Baptiste De Marbot*—A French Cavalryman Of the Napoleonic Wars at Marengo, Austerlitz, Jena, Eylau & Friedland.

THE LIFE OF THE REAL BRIGADIER GERARD VOLUME 2—IMPERIAL AIDE-DE-CAMP 1807-1811 *by Jean-Baptiste De Marbot*—A French Cavalryman of the Napoleonic Wars at Saragossa, Landshut, Eckmuhl, Ratisbon, Aspern-Essling, Wagram, Busaco & Torres Vedras.

THE LIFE OF THE REAL BRIGADIER GERARD VOLUME 3—COLONEL OF CHASSEURS 1811-1815 *by Jean-Baptiste De Marbot*—A French Cavalryman in the retreat from Moscow, Lutzen, Bautzen, Katzbach, Leipzig, Hanau & Waterloo.

THE INDIAN WAR OF 1864 *by Eugene Ware*—The Experiences of a Young Officer of the 7th Iowa Cavalry on the Western Frontier During the Civil War.

THE MARCH OF DESTINY *by Charles E. Young & V. Devinny*—Dangers of the Trail in 1865 by Charles E. Young & The Story of a Pioneer by V. Devinny, two Accounts of Early Emigrants to Colorado.

CROSSING THE PLAINS *by William Audley Maxwell*—A First Hand Narrative of the Early Pioneer Trail to California in 1857.

CHIEF OF SCOUTS *by William F. Drannan*—A Pilot to Emigrant and Government Trains, Across the Plains of the Western Frontier.

THIRTY-ONE YEARS ON THE PLAINS AND IN THE MOUNTAINS *by William F. Drannan*—William Drannan was born to be a pioneer, hunter, trapper and wagon train guide during the momentous days of the Great American West.

THE INDIAN WARS VOLUNTEER *by William Thompson*—Recollections of the Conflict Against the Snakes, Shoshone, Bannocks, Modocs and Other Native Tribes of the American North West.

THE 4TH TENNESSEE CAVALRY *by George B. Guild*—The Services of Smith's Regiment of Confederate Cavalry by One of its Officers.

COLONEL WORTHINGTON'S SHILOH *by T. Worthington*—The Tennessee Campaign, 1862, by an Officer of the Ohio Volunteers.

FOUR YEARS IN THE SADDLE *by W. L. Curry*—The History of the First Regiment Ohio Volunteer Cavalry in the American Civil War.

www.ingramcontent.com/pod-product-compliance
Lightning Source LLC
Chambersburg PA
CBHW031858090426

42741CB00005B/548